D1280667

Writing Empirical Research Reports

A Basic Guide for Students of the Social and Behavioral Sciences

Fifth Edition

Fred Pyrczak

California State University, Los Angeles

Randall R. Bruce

Editorial Consultant

Pyrczak Publishing

P.O. Box 250430 • Glendale, CA 91225

"Pyrczak Publishing" is an imprint of Fred Pyrczak, Publisher, A California Corporation.

Although the author and publisher have made every effort to ensure the accuracy and completeness of information contained in this book, we assume no responsibility for errors, inaccuracies, omissions, or any inconsistency herein. Any slights of people, places, or organizations are unintentional.

Project Director: Monica Lopez.

Editorial assistance provided by Kenneth Ornburn, Brenda Koplin, Sharon Young, Erica Simmons, and Cheryl Alcorn.

Cover design by Robert Kibler and Larry Nichols.

Printed in the United States of America by Malloy, Inc.

Copyright © 2005, 2003, 2000, 1998, 1992 by Pyrczak Publishing. All rights reserved. Permission is hereby granted for professors and their students to photocopy Appendix A for use only in classes in which this book is used as a required textbook. Except for Appendix A, no portion of this book may be reproduced or transmitted in any form or by any means without the prior written permission of the publisher.

ISBN 1-884585-58-2

Contents

Notes:

Introduction to the Fifth Edition

This book presents guidelines frequently followed by writers of empirical research reports. The guidelines describe the types of information that should be included, how this information should be expressed, and where various types of information should be placed within a research report.

Students whose professors require them to write research-based term papers that resemble journal articles will find this book useful. The exercises at the end of each chapter are designed for their use. Graduate students who are writing theses and dissertations will find that most of the guidelines also apply to their writing. Interspersed throughout the text are pointers for such students. Finally, students who are writing research proposals will also find that most of the guidelines apply to their writing.

What This Book Will *Not* Do for You

This book is not a traditional style manual that prescribes mechanical details such as the forms for levels of headings, typing requirements, and so on. A number of excellent style manuals, including the *Publication Manual of the American Psychological Association*, already cover these matters. Neither will you find here a discussion of the mechanics of standard English usage; it is assumed that you have already mastered these. Finally, it is also assumed that you have already selected an important research topic, applied sound research methods, and analyzed the data. Thus, these topics are not covered.

Cautions in Using This Book

The guidelines presented in this book are based on generalizations that we reached while reading extensively in journals in the social and behavioral sciences. If you are a student using this book in a research class, your professor may ask you to ignore or modify some of the guidelines you will find here. This may occur for two reasons. First, as a learning experience, your professor may require you to do certain things that go beyond the preparation of a paper for possible publication. For example, we suggest that the literature review for a journal article should usually be highly selective. Your professor may have you write a more extensive literature review, however, in order for you to show that you know how to conduct a comprehensive search of the literature on a topic. Second, as in all types of writing, there is a certain amount of subjectivity concerning what constitutes effective writing; even experts differ. Fortunately, these differences are less pronounced in scientific writing than in many other types.

Experienced writers may violate many of the guidelines presented in this book and still write effective research reports that are publishable. Beginners are encouraged to follow the guidelines rather closely until they have mastered the art of scientific writing.

Where to Begin in This Book

For a quick overview of five fundamental principles for effective research writing, begin with Appendix B, *Thinking Straight and Writing That Way*. Then read Chapter 1, which will provide an overview of the structure of typical research reports.

About the Fifth Edition

The most important change from the Fourth to the Fifth Edition is the addition of two new chapters: Chapter 1 on structuring a research report and Chapter 14 on preparing a reference list.

All the guidelines that were in the Fourth Edition are included in this one. You will find that many of the examples that illustrate the guidelines have been updated with newer ones that deal with contemporary issues. In addition to the new guidelines in the two new chapters, the following new guidelines are included in other chapters in this edition: 2.2, 2.7, 6.7, 6.8, 6.20, 9.6, 9.7, 13.8, 13.10, and 13.11.

Acknowledgments

The authors are grateful to Dr. Dean Purcell of Oakland University, who provided many helpful comments on the First Edition of this book. Dr. Robert Morman of California State University, Los Angeles, provided many useful suggestions. Any errors, of course, remain the responsibility of the authors.

Chapter 1

Structuring a Research Report

This chapter provides an overview of the elements typically included in research reports. Each of these is discussed in greater detail in later chapters.

➢ Guideline 1.1   A research report typically has a brief title.

Titles of published research reports typically are brief. They usually refer to the population of interest and to the variables studied. Example 1.1.1 shows a title of about average length for a research report published in an academic journal. In it, the variables are self-concept and employment status. The population consists of individuals with epilepsy.

Example 1.1.1
The Relationship Between Self-Concept and Employment Status Among Individuals with Epilepsy

Chapter 5 in this book covers how to write titles in more detail.

➢ Guideline 1.2   An abstract usually follows the title.

An abstract is a brief summary of the research. It is often stated in as few as 150 words or less. Its purpose is to help individuals who are searching for literature quickly identify research reports of particular interest to them. Abstracts are especially important to such individuals because abstracts are more informative than titles.

An abstract should normally be written after the body of the report has been completed. Hence, guidelines for writing them are presented near the end of this book in Chapter 12.

➢ Guideline 1.3   The body of a basic research report should have an introduction that includes a literature review, a section on research methods, a section on results, and a discussion.

The elements specified in this guideline are almost always covered in the order in which they are named. For instance, the introduction and literature review almost always precede the section describing the research methods that were employed to conduct the study.

Writing introductions and literature reviews is covered in Chapter 6, writing method sections is covered in Chapter 9, writing analysis and results sections is covered in Chapter 10, and writing discussion sections is covered in Chapter 11.

➢ Guideline 1.4   The section on research methods almost always has two main subsections: "Participants" and "Instrumentation."

The subsection on the participants describes how they were identified and selected. The subsection on instrumentation describes the measuring tools, such as tests and attitude scales.

While there may be variations in wording of the subheadings (such as "Sample" instead of "Participants" or "Measures" instead of "Instrumentation"), these two subsections are almost always included in the method section. Chapter 9 describes guidelines for writing method sections.

Example 1.4.1 shows the structure of a basic research report with the elements discussed up to this point in this chapter.

Example 1.4.1

Title in Upper- and Lower-Case Letters
Abstract
An introduction including a literature review (typically with no heading)
Method (a main heading that is centered)
Participants (a subheading that is flush left)
Instrumentation (a subheading that is flush left)
Results (a main heading that is centered)
Discussion (a main heading that is centered)

A third subheading, "Procedure," is sometimes included under "Instrumentation" in the Method section. This is the appropriate place to describe the treatments given in an experiment, including details such as which participants received each treatment, who administered the treatments, and how long the treatments lasted.

Normally, researchers do not describe how they computed widely used statistics. However, when they use new statistical methods or when they have chosen a lesser known method of analysis over a more commonly used one, it is appropriate to label the results section with the main heading of "Analysis and Results" instead of just "Results."

➢ Guideline 1.5   Be generous in using subheadings within each main section of the report.

Subheadings help readers follow the structure of a research report. Also, researchers often find that using subheadings that break up each major section of a research report into manageable shorter subsections makes writing a research report easier.

Example 1.5.1 shows the structure of a research report with a number of subheadings.

Example 1.5.1

Title

Abstract

An introduction that begins here without a heading, followed by a literature review with the following subheadings.

Pervasiveness of the Problem[1]
Conflicts in the Literature
Gaps in the Literature
Theoretical Perspectives
Rationale for Hypothesis 1
Rationale for Hypothesis 2

Method

Participants
   Identifying the Population
   Selecting the Sample
   Demographics of the Sample
Instrumentation
   The Achievement Test

---

[1] This is the first subheading within the integrated introduction and literature review. It would be preceded by one or more paragraphs that provide a general introduction to the research topic.

> *The Attitude Scale*
> **Procedure**
>   *Assignment to the Treatments*
>   *Administration of the Treatments*
>
> Results
>
> **Results for Hypothesis 1**
>   *Descriptive Statistics*
>   *Significance Tests*
> **Results for Hypothesis 2**
>   *Descriptive Statistics*
>   *Significance Tests*
>
> Discussion
>
> **Summary**
> **Implications**
>   *Implications for Clinical Psychologists*
>   *Theoretical Implications*
> **Limitations of the Current Research**
> **Suggestions for Future Research**
> **Conclusions**

Note that the number of subheadings and their names can vary greatly depending on the topic and the research methods used. Also note that the research hypotheses, research objectives, or research questions are typically stated just before the Method section, as is done in Example 1.5.1 above (e.g., "Rationale for Hypothesis 1"). Writing research hypotheses, objectives, questions, and purposes is covered in Chapters 2, 3, and 4.

Example 1.5.2 shows the headings and subheadings used in a recently published research report. Note that the paragraph under the title in italics is the complete abstract. Only portions of the text are shown under each of the headings and subheadings.

Example 1.5.2

Adolescent Mothers in a Transitional Living Facility:
An Exploratory Study of Support Networks and Attachment Patterns

Most of the research literature on attachment and adolescent transitions has addressed youth in family settings. This article explores these issues with a sample of 25 pregnant and parenting teens living in a transitional shelter. Using case records and interview data as well as results of standardized measures of depression, self-esteem, child abuse potential, and emotional autonomy, insights on relationships between adolescent mothers and their parents, romantic partners, staff, and children are explored, and implications are provided for agencies serving this population.

[Note: The introduction to the report begins here without a heading.]

According to psychoanalytic theory, the processes of separation and individuation are the main tasks of adolescence and the transition to young adulthood (Kenny, 1994). However, Bowlby (1988) and Ainsworth (1989) have long held that attachment is a lifelong need, not something children outgrow. Even as individuals achieve a high degree of autonomy and establish....[2]

Attachment Theory[3]

At the heart of attachment theory is the primacy of intimate bonds for human functioning (Bowlby, 1988). Unlike psychoanalytic theory, attachment theory states that emotional bonds are....

Attachment and Adolescence

According to attachment theorists, the developmental changes of adolescence do not have an impact on attachment patterns. Adolescents face....

The Importance of Attachment for Adolescents

Insecure parental attachments have been correlated with a number of negative outcomes in adolescents. Allen et al. (1996) found....

The Influence of Teen Pregnancy on Attachment

Limited research has been conducted on the attachment relationships of adolescent mothers. Many of these women confront....

Research Questions

Using Bowlby's theoretical perspective on attachment, this study was designed to explore....

The literature on attachment theory suggested the following [research] questions for the population under study:

What is the nature of the attachments between....

What outcomes do participants exhibit that may be related to....

What outcomes do participants' children exhibit that may be related to....

Method

Participants[4]

The sample for this study consisted of 25 adolescent mothers participating in the first 18 months of a transitional living program located....

Instrumentation

Qualitative Measures. This study is based on a comprehensive analysis of multiple data sources used by researchers in....

Quantitative Measures. Several standardized measures were used to assess participants' emotional well-being and....

Results

Relationships with Parents

For most of the participants, relationships with parents have been tenuous and often disrupted. For some, their parental relationships have been....

---

[2] This paragraph is the beginning of the integrated introduction and literature review. It begins directly under the abstract without a heading.

[3] This is the first subheading within the integrated introduction and literature review. It indicates that the literature on attachment theory will be discussed in this section.

[4] This is the first subheading under "Method."

Romantic Relationships

A majority of these adolescent participants indicated that they either had a boyfriend or were currently....

Relationships with Children

Because the participants have experienced insecure attachments with their own early attachment figures and face many challenges to....

Discussion

Although it is impossible to generalize or draw strong conclusions from....

References

Ainsworth, M. (1989). Attachments beyond infancy. *American Psychologist, 44,*....[5]

➢ Guideline 1.6   In a thesis or dissertation, the introduction and the literature review are often presented in separate chapters.

Unlike journal articles in which the literature review is typically integrated into the introduction, theses and dissertations typically have two separate chapters for these elements. Chapter 1 presents the introduction, which defines the topic of the research and establishes its importance, and Chapter 2 provides a synthesis of the literature on the topic.

If you are writing a research report for a class, check with your instructor on whether you should write a separate introduction or write an introduction that integrates the literature review within it.

Concluding Comments

The essential elements in a research report are the title, abstract, introduction, literature review, a description of research methods, a section that presents results, and a discussion. Additional headings and subheadings may be used as needed for clarity or presentation.

Note that researchers also present definitions as well as descriptions of their assumptions, limitations, and delimitations in their research reports. These elements may be integrated within various sections of a report or may be presented in separate sections. Guidelines for writing these elements are presented in Chapters 7 and 8.

---

[5] Example 1.5.2 is loosely based on Schwartz, McRoy, & Downs (2004).

Exercise for Chapter 1

PART A

1. "Titles of published research reports typically are very lengthy." According to this chapter, is this statement true *or* false?

2. Is the abstract usually placed above *or* below the title?

3. "An abstract is an extensive summary of the research." According to this chapter, is this statement true *or* false?

4. What are the two main subsections that are almost always included within the section on research methods?

5. According to this chapter, should subheadings be used sparingly *or* should they be used generously?

6. Are the introduction and literature review always integrated into a single section? Explain.

PART B: Examine two reports of research published in journals, and answer the following questions.

7. Were the titles and abstracts brief *or* lengthy? Explain.

8. Were the headings and subheadings consistent with what you expected based on your reading of this chapter? Explain.

PART C: If you will be writing a thesis or dissertation in the near future, examine two of them, and answer the following questions.

9. Were the introductions and literature reviews presented in separate chapters?

10. Were the headings and subheadings consistent with what you expected based on your reading of this chapter? Explain.

Notes:

Chapter 2

Writing Simple Research Hypotheses

In a single sentence, a simple research hypothesis describes the results that a researcher expects to find. In effect, it is a prediction. The following are guidelines for writing this type of hypothesis.

➤ Guideline 2.1   A simple research hypothesis should name two variables and indicate the type of relationship expected between them.

In Example 2.1.1, the variables are "psychomotor coordination" and "self-esteem." The researcher expects to find higher self-esteem among individuals who have more psychomotor coordination and lower self-esteem among those who have less coordination. Note that the word "positive" may be substituted for "direct" without changing the meaning of the hypothesis.

Example 2.1.1   *or +*

There is a direct relationship between level of psychomotor coordination and degree of self-esteem.

In Example 2.1.2, "length of light deprivation" is a stimulus or *independent variable*, which will be manipulated by the researcher. The hypothesis suggests that some rats will be deprived of light longer than others will. The second variable is "performance in a maze task," which is an outcome or *dependent variable*. The hypothesis indicates that the researcher expects to find longer periods of light deprivation associated with poorer maze performance.

Example 2.1.2

Among rats, length of light deprivation from birth is inversely associated with performance in a maze task.

Example 2.1.3 also contains an independent variable: the type of paper given to teachers. The anticipated relationship of this variable to the willingness of teachers to accept learning-disabled students is clear in the hypothesis. Their willingness to have learning-disabled students in their classrooms is the dependent variable.

Example 2.1.3

Teachers who are given a paper containing practical tips on teaching learning-disabled students will be more willing to have such students in their classrooms than teachers who are given a theoretical paper on learning disabilities.

In Example 2.1.4, two variables are named, but the expected relationship between them is not stated. The Improved Version of Example 2.1.4 makes it clear that the researcher believes that those with more free-floating anxiety have less ability to form friendships.

Example 2.1.4

College students differ in their levels of free-floating anxiety, and they differ in their ability to form friendships.

Improved Version of Example 2.1.4

Among college students, there is an inverse relationship between level of free-floating anxiety and ability to form friendships.

Note that in the Improved Version of Example 2.1.4, the word "negative" could be substituted for "inverse" without changing the meaning of the hypothesis.

➢ Guideline 2.2   When there is an independent variable, name a specific dependent variable.

As you know from the previous guideline, some studies have independent variables, which are sets of treatments that are manipulated by the researchers. The outcome that results from a set of treatments is known as the dependent variable. The purpose of such a study (known as an *experiment*) is to determine the effects of the independent variable on the dependent variable.[1] The hypothesis for an experiment should name a

---

[1] A study without an independent variable such as one investigating the relationship between participants' gender and voting behavior (in which, of course, neither gender nor voting behavior are treatments that will be given by the researcher) is known as a *nonexperimental study*.

specific dependent variable. In Example 2.2.1, the independent variable is the use of guest speakers. Furthermore, the term "more effective" implies that there is a dependent variable, which is not specified. The improved version specifies that the dependent variable is the number of career choices considered by the participants.

Example 2.2.1

Career counseling supplemented with guest speakers holding various occupations will be more effective than career counseling without guest speakers.

Improved Version of Example 2.2.1

Participants receiving career counseling supplemented with guest speakers holding various occupations will report that they have considered a larger number of career choices than participants who receive career counseling without guest speakers.

Because the purpose of all experiments is to determine the *effects* of the independent variable on a dependent variable, it is never sufficiently specific to state only that the dependent variable is the "effects" or any variation on this term such as "more effective."

Example 2.2.2 also fails to name a specific dependent variable. The improved version specifies that "lower blood-pressure readings" is the dependent variable.

Example 2.2.2

Middle-aged males who regularly exercise vigorously will be better off than those who do not exercise vigorously.

Improved Version of Example 2.2.2

Middle-aged males who regularly exercise vigorously will have lower blood-pressure readings than those who do not exercise vigorously.

➢ Guideline 2.3   When a relationship is expected only in a particular population, consider naming the population in the hypothesis.

In Example 2.3.1, "young children" are identified as the researcher's population of interest.

Example 2.3.1

Among young children, there is a direct relationship between level of psychomotor coordination and degree of self-esteem.

In Example 2.3.2, "student nurses" are identified as the researcher's population of interest.

Example 2.3.2

Student nurses who receive computer-assisted training in calculating drug dosages will make fewer calculation errors than student nurses who do not receive computer-assisted training.

➢ Guideline 2.4   A simple hypothesis should be as specific as possible, yet expressed in a single sentence.

The hypothesis in Example 2.4.1 violates this guideline because it is stated in two sentences. This is corrected in the improved version.

Example 2.4.1

Social anxiety may impede the speech-giving performance of college students in speech communication classes. As a result, students with such anxiety will perform more poorly in such classes.

Improved Version of Example 2.4.1

Students with high levels of social anxiety will exhibit poorer speech-giving performance than students with low levels of social anxiety.

The Improved Version of Example 2.4.2 is more specific than the original because the meanings of "computer literacy" (i.e., training in the use of computers) and "computer use" (i.e., number of administrative tasks they perform using computers) are indicated in the improved version.

Example 2.4.2

There is a direct relationship between administrators' computer literacy and their computer use.

Improved Version of Example 2.4.2

Among administrators, there is a direct relationship between the amount of training they have had in the use of computers and the number of administrative tasks they perform using computers.

Likewise, the Improved Version of Example 2.4.3 is more specific than the original version because the improved version indicates that being "better administrators" will be measured in terms of employees' perceptions of leadership qualities. Also, the improved version is more specific because it indicates that two types of administrators will be compared.

Example 2.4.3

Administrators who provide wellness programs for their employees will be better administrators.

Improved Version of Example 2.4.3

Administrators who provide wellness programs for their employees will receive higher employee ratings on selected leadership qualities than administrators who do not provide wellness programs.

Deciding how specific to make a hypothesis requires good judgment because it is usually not possible to provide full definitions of all terms in the single sentence that states a hypothesis. Instead, complete definitions should be provided elsewhere in a research report. Guidelines for writing definitions are presented in Chapter 7.

➤ Guideline 2.5   If a comparison is to be made, the elements to be compared should be stated.

Comparisons start with terms such as "more," "less," "higher," and "lower." Be sure to complete any comparisons you start with these terms. The comparison that is started in Example 2.5.1 is not complete, forcing the reader to make an assumption about the group(s) to which the low-achieving students will be compared. The improved versions are superior because they complete the comparison that starts with the word *more*. Note that the improved versions illustrate that the comparison can be completed in more than one way, clearly showing that the original version is vague.

Example 2.5.1

Low-achieving primary-grade students are more dependent on adults for psychological support.

Improved Versions of Example 2.5.1

Low-achieving primary-grade students are more dependent on adults for psychological support than average achievers.

Low-achieving primary-grade students are more dependent on adults for psychological support than high achievers.

Low-achieving primary-grade students are more dependent on adults for psychological support than average and high achievers.

➢ Guideline 2.6   Because most hypotheses deal with the behavior of groups, plural forms should usually be used.

In Example 2.6.1, singular terms are used to refer to the participants (i.e., "a husband" and "a wife"). Because the hypothesis will undoubtedly be tested using groups of husbands and wives, the improved version of the hypothesis is preferable.

Example 2.6.1

Retirement satisfaction will be greater when a husband or a wife has greater marital satisfaction than when he or she has less marital satisfaction.

Improved Version of Example 2.6.1

Married individuals who have greater marital satisfaction will have greater retirement satisfaction than those who have less marital satisfaction.

➢ Guideline 2.7   Avoid sex-role stereotypes in the statement of a hypothesis.

In Example 2.7.1, use of the term "her level" reflects the sex-role stereotype that nursing is an occupation for women only. The problem has been corrected in the improved version by substituting the plural terms "nurses" and "their level." Of course, it is important to avoid sex-role stereotyping throughout research reports.

Example 2.7.1

There is a direct relationship between a nurse's participation in administrative decision making and her level of job satisfaction.

Improved Version of Example 2.7.1

There is a direct relationship between nurses' participation in administrative decision making and their level of job satisfaction.

➢ Guideline 2.8   A hypothesis should be free of terms and phrases that do not add to its meaning.

The Improved Version of Example 2.8.1 is much shorter than the original version, yet its meaning is clear.

Example 2.8.1

Among elementary school teachers, those who are teaching in year-round schools will report having higher morale than those who are teaching in elementary schools that follow a more traditional school-year schedule.

Improved Version of Example 2.8.1

Elementary school teachers who teach in year-round schools will report having higher morale than those who teach on a traditional schedule.

➢ Guideline 2.9   A hypothesis should indicate what will actually be studied—not the possible implications of a study or value judgments of the author.

In Example 2.9.1, the author is expressing a value judgment rather than the anticipated relationship between the variables to be studied. The improved version indicates how "religion" will be treated as a variable (i.e., attendance at religious services) and indicates the specific outcome (i.e., cheating behavior) that will be studied.

Example 2.9.1

Religion is good for society.

Improved Version of Example 2.9.1

Attendance at religious services is inversely associated with students' cheating behavior while taking classroom tests.

Note that if the hypothesis in the Improved Version of Example 2.9.1 is supported by the data generated to test the hypothesis, the researcher may want to assert that less cheating is "good for society" in his or her research report. Such an assertion is acceptable as long as the researcher makes it clear that the assertion is a value judgment and not a data-based conclusion.

➤ Guideline 2.10   A hypothesis usually should name variables in the order in which they occur or will be measured.

In Example 2.10.1, the natural order has been reversed because the deprivation will precede, and possibly produce, the anticipated anxiety. This problem has been corrected in the improved version.

Example 2.10.1

More free-floating anxiety will be observed among adults who are subjected to longer periods of sensory deprivation.

Improved Version of Example 2.10.1

Adults who are subjected to extended periods of sensory deprivation will experience more free-floating anxiety than those exposed to less deprivation.

In Example 2.10.2, the natural order has been reversed. Because political advertising precedes winning elections, advertisements should be mentioned before election to office. The problem has been corrected in the improved version.

Example 2.10.2

Politicians who win elective offices tend to focus their political advertisements on a limited number of issues while those who lose elections tend to focus on a larger number of issues.

Improved Version of Example 2.10.2

Politicians who focus their political advertisements on a limited number of issues are more likely to win elective office than those whose advertisements cover a larger number of issues.

Of course, we would expect the researcher to define at some point in the research report what is meant by "limited number" and "larger number."

➢ Guideline 2.11 Avoid using the words "significant" or "significance" in a hypothesis.

The terms "significant" and "significance" usually refer to tests of statistical significance. Because most empirical studies include these tests, reference to them in hypotheses is not necessary; knowledgeable readers will assume that the issue of statistical significance will be dealt with in the results section of a quantitative research report.

➢ Guideline 2.12 Avoid using the word "prove" in a hypothesis.

Empirical research does not *prove* its outcomes for three primary reasons. First, empirical research is usually based only on samples from populations, and it is safe to assume that no sample is perfectly representative of its population. Second, it is safe to assume that no test or other measurement procedure is perfectly valid and reliable. Finally, it is always possible that research has been influenced by unintentional biases. These biases can take an infinitive variety of forms, such as unintentionally testing the control group in a noisier environment than the one used for testing the experimental group *or* a research assistant unintentionally suggesting answers to respondents (without the researcher's knowledge) in an opinion survey. Thus, researchers should not naively set out to *prove* something with empirical research methods. Instead, they should recognize that they will be collecting data that offer varying degrees of confidence regarding various conclusions. The greater the degree of care taken in reducing errors, the more confidence in the results researchers are justified in having.

➢ Guideline 2.13 Avoid using two different terms to refer to the same variable in a hypothesis.

In Example 2.13.1, it is not clear whether the "literature-based approach" is the same as the "new approach" because two different terms are being used. This problem has been corrected in the improved version.

Example 2.13.1

Students who receive a literature-based approach to reading instruction plus training in phonetics will have better attitudes toward reading than those who receive only the new approach to reading instruction.

Improved Version of Example 2.13.1

Students who receive a literature-based approach to reading instruction plus training in phonetics will have better attitudes toward reading than those who receive only the literature-based approach to reading instruction.

Note that clarity of communication is of utmost importance in scientific writing. Varying the terms used to refer to a single construct, as one might do in creative writing, is likely to impede clear scientific communication.

➤ Guideline 2.14   Avoid making precise statistical predictions in a hypothesis.

Precise statistical predictions are rarely justified. In addition, they may make it almost impossible to confirm a hypothesis. Consider Example 2.14.1. If contamination were reduced by any percentage other than 35, the hypothesis would have to be rejected. For example, if there was a 99% reduction in bacterial contamination, the hypothesis would need to be rejected because it is more than 35%. Likewise, if there was a 1% reduction, the hypothesis would also need to be rejected because it is less than 35%. The improved version indicates the direction of the expected relationship without naming a precise statistical outcome.

Example 2.14.1

Thirty-five percent less bacterial contamination will be found in the air of operating rooms in which the staff wears polypropylene coveralls than in the air of operating rooms in which they wear conventional surgical clothing.

Improved Version of Example 2.14.1

Less bacterial contamination will be found in the air of operating rooms in which the staff wears polypropylene coveralls than in the air of operating rooms in which they wear conventional surgical clothing.

Exercise for Chapter 2

Because the application of many of the guidelines in this chapter involves a certain amount of subjectivity, there may be some legitimate differences of opinions on the best answers to some of the following questions.

PART A: Name the two variables in each of the following hypotheses.

1. There is an inverse relationship between ability to read and frequency of voting among elderly citizens.

2. Among college graduates, authoritarianism and anxiety are directly related.

3. Homeless women are subjected to more spousal physical abuse than are housed women.

4. Children who are shown a film with numerous instances of physical violence will demonstrate more aggressiveness during a free play period than children who are shown a control film without violence.

5. Among first graders, there is a direct relationship between level of eye–hand coordination and achievement in volleyball.

6. Among adolescents, interest in recreational reading is inversely associated with amount of time spent watching television.

PART B: For each of the following hypotheses, identify the *independent variable* and the *dependent variable*. (See pages 9 through 11 to review these terms.)

7. Negative political advertisements are more likely to motivate citizens to vote in general elections than positive advertisements.

8. Disruptive children who are given token rewards for remaining in their seats in a classroom setting will exhibit more in-seat behavior than disruptive children who are given verbal praise.

9. Postcardiac adults who receive telephone counseling to encourage engaging in physical exercise will report walking more miles per day than postcardiac adults who do not receive the telephone counseling.

PART C: For each of the following hypotheses, name the guideline(s), if any, that were not followed. Revise each hypothesis that you think is faulty. In your revisions, you may need to make some assumptions about what the authors had in mind when writing the hypotheses.

10. The hypothesis is to prove that first-born boys are more athletically competitive than are second-born boys.

11. Children differ in age, and they also differ in their ability to attend to instructional presentations.

12. The rate of development of speech in young children is directly related to the verbal fluency of their parents.

13. Among high achievers, there will be a higher level of sibling rivalry.

14. An individual who experiences marital dissatisfaction will tend to be more depressed than an individual who experiences marital satisfaction.

15. Other things being equal, more rewards result in better performance.

16. The social agenda of the present administration is weak.

17. There is a direct relationship between a mechanical engineer's ability to visualize objects rotating in space and his success on the job.

18. Fifty percent of employees with poor attendance records will be found to have alcohol-related syndromes.

19. College applicants who take test preparation courses will exhibit less test-taking anxiety.

20. First graders whose parents read to them on a regular basis will have greater reading achievement.

21. Students who take Psychology 101 will report less self-insight on a questionnaire given at the beginning of the course than on a posttest given at the end of an introduction to psychology course.

22. People who cheat the welfare system are disreputable.

23. There will be a 25% reduction in the incidence of smoking after high school students complete a unit on the harmful effects of tobacco.

24. Using discussion groups in college sociology classes will be more effective than a traditional lecture approach to instruction.

PART D: Write a simple hypothesis on a topic of interest to you that includes an independent and a dependent variable. Then name the variables in the spaces provided.

Your hypothesis:

Independent variable:

Dependent variable:

PART E: Write a simple hypothesis on a topic of interest to you that does *not* have independent and dependent variables. Mention a population in the hypothesis.

Your hypothesis:

The population:

Notes:

Chapter 3

A Closer Look at Hypotheses

This chapter presents some advanced guidelines for writing hypotheses and explores some of the principles from Chapter 1 in greater detail.

➢ Guideline 3.1   A "statement of the hypothesis" may contain more than one hypothesis. It is permissible to include them in a single sentence as long as the sentence is reasonably concise and its meaning is clear.

In Example 3.1.1, there is one independent variable (supplementary group therapy) and two anticipated outcomes or dependent variables. Therefore, there are two hypotheses: (1) those who receive the group therapy supplement will report more relief and (2) those who receive the group therapy supplement will be more satisfied with the counseling process.

Example 3.1.1

Depressed clients whose individual counseling is supplemented with group therapy will report more relief from their symptoms and greater satisfaction with the counseling process than comparable clients who receive only individual counseling.

➢ Guideline 3.2   When a number of related hypotheses are to be stated, consider presenting them in a numbered or lettered list.

Example 3.2.1 shows three related hypotheses stated by researchers for a study of social learning theory.

Example 3.2.1

It was hypothesized that adolescent high school students' desire to learn academic subjects will be more greatly influenced by:

1. same-gender peers than opposite-gender peers,
2. peers who are elected to student-body positions than those who have not been elected, and
3. peers who have excelled in nonacademic areas such as sports than those who have not excelled.

Such a numbered list will be helpful when writing other sections of the research report. For instance, when discussing research results, researchers can make statements such as the ones shown in Examples 3.2.2 and 3.2.3. Notice that numbering the hypotheses early in a research report makes it easy to clearly refer to a specific hypothesis without having to restate the entire hypothesis. In Example 3.2.2, this was done with a parenthetical phrase; in Example 3.2.3, there is no parenthetical phrase. Either form is correct. However, modern copyeditors discourage the overuse of parentheses.

Example 3.2.2

Regarding the first hypothesis (same- versus opposite-gender influence), the results are clear. The mean score for the….

Example 3.2.3

Regarding the influence of same- versus opposite-gender peers specified in Hypothesis Number 1, the results are clear. The mean score for the….

➤ Guideline 3.3   The hypothesis or hypotheses should be placed before the section on methods.

The method section of a research report describes how the researcher tested the hypothesis. Therefore, the hypothesis should be stated before describing the methods used.

In journal articles, hypotheses are usually stated in the paragraph immediately preceding the major heading of "Method," which is the last paragraph of the integrated introduction and literature review (see Chapter 6). In theses and dissertations, the placement is usually at the end of the second chapter, which is the literature review. (In a thesis or dissertation, the first chapter is usually the introduction, while the second chapter is the literature review.) Placement of hypotheses may vary from institution to institution. Before you begin writing, determine the specific guidelines for your university or department.

➢ Guideline 3.4   It is permissible to use terms other than the term "hypothesis" to refer to a hypothesis.

The context and placement of the statement just before the method section usually make it clear that a hypothesis is being stated even if the word "hypothesis" is not used. In Example 3.4.1, the researchers describe two *expectations*, which were their hypotheses.

Example 3.4.1

Based on prior research, we expected that the effects of religiosity on the decision to use alcohol and on the intensity of involvement in drinking will be strong even when controlling for peer, family, and school influences.[1]

Other writers begin the statements of their hypotheses with phrases such as "In light of the literature review, it was predicted that…" and "We speculated that…." Generally, however, it is best to use the formal term "hypothesis" or "hypothesized" in phrases such as: "In light of the literature review, it was hypothesized that…" or "The hypothesis is that…."

Note that in a research proposal, the present tense should be used (e.g., "The hypothesis is…") while in a research report, the past tense is usually more appropriate (e.g., "The hypothesis was…").

➢ Guideline 3.5   In a research report, a hypothesis should flow from the narrative that immediately precedes it.

A research report typically begins with an introduction and literature review, which we will consider in detail in Chapter 6. These elements of a report should logically lead the reader to the hypothesis. Example 3.5.1 is drawn from the last paragraph in a combined introduction and literature review. Prior to stating this hypothesis, the researchers discuss the increase in adolescents' rates of smoking cigarettes, research on the use of

---

[1] Based loosely on the work of Mason & Windle (2002, p. 350).

visual imagery in advertising, and theories relating to the influence of strong positive images in advertisements for cigarettes as well as the efficacy of cigarette advertisements. The hypothesis in this example clearly flows directly from the researchers' discussion of these issues.

Example 3.5.1

Given the seeming efficacy of cigarette advertisements in promoting smoking uptake by adolescents and the seeming inefficacy of antismoking advertising in preventing smoking uptake, we hypothesized that cigarette advertising imagery would be evaluated more positively than antismoking advertising imagery. Confirmation of this hypothesis would suggest that antismoking advertisements may need to be reconceptualized and redesigned so that they are perceived more positively by adolescents.[2]

Note that Example 3.5.1 ends with a broadly stated possible implication, which helps to justify a study to the hypothesis.

➢ Guideline 3.6   A hypothesis may be stated without indicating the type of relationship expected between variables. To qualify as a hypothesis, however, it must specify that some unknown type of relationship is expected.

A hypothesis that states that an unknown type of relationship exists is called a *nondirectional hypothesis*. (Up to this point in this book, all the hypotheses have been *directional*.) Example 3.6.1 illustrates a *nondirectional hypothesis* for a nonexperimental study. Notice that the hypothesis does *not* indicate which group of police officers is predicted to be higher in its level of authoritarianism; it just states that the two groups differ. Also, note that it implies that a nonexperimental study will be conducted because no treatments will be given to the officers in order to influence their authoritarianism.

---

[2] Shadel, Niaura, & Abrams (2002, pp. 173–174).

Example 3.6.1

Police officers reared in low socioeconomic status families differ in their level of authoritarianism from police officers reared in middle socioeconomic-status families.[3]

Example 3.6.2 shows a nondirectional hypothesis for an experimental study, in which Drugs A and B are the treatments that will be administered in the experiment.

Example 3.6.2

Adult males with Condition X who are administered Drug A will, on average, report a different level of pain than a comparable group of males who are administered Drug B.

Nondirectional hypotheses are less frequently used in research than directional hypotheses. This is probably true for two reasons: (1) researchers often have opinions about the variables they study, and their opinions usually lead them to formulate directional hypotheses, and (2) when researchers do not want to speculate on the direction of a relationship, they may use a statement of the research purpose or a research question instead of a hypothesis. This type of substitution is discussed in detail in Chapter 4.

➢ Guideline 3.7   When a researcher has a research hypothesis, it should be stated in the research report; the null hypothesis need not always be stated.

A *research hypothesis* is the hypothesis that a researcher believes will be supported by his or her data. The *null hypothesis* is a *statistical hypothesis* that states that any difference is attributable to random errors. In other words, it says that there is no true difference—only a random one. Significance tests are used to test the null hypothesis. (Those of you who have not taken a statistics course should consult Appendix C for an introduction to the null hypothesis and significance testing.)

In journal articles, formal statements of null hypotheses are almost always omitted because they always have the same content—regardless of

---

[3] An example of a *directional hypothesis* for the same variables is "Police officers reared in low socioeconomic status families are more authoritarian than police officers reared in middle socioeconomic status families."

how they are worded (i.e., they always attribute any differences to random errors). Thus, it would be redundant to repeatedly state the null hypothesis in all quantitative research reports.

In term projects, theses, and dissertations, however, students are often required to state null hypotheses in order to demonstrate that they understand the purpose of the significance tests they conducted. (The purpose, as you may know, is to test the null hypothesis.) Examples 3.7.1 and 3.7.2 illustrate some ways the null hypothesis can be stated. Because there is more than one way to word a null hypothesis, two statements are shown in each example. Only one statement, however, should be used in a research report.

Example 3.7.1

RESEARCH HYPOTHESIS:

Social standing in campus organizations is directly related to gregariousness.

ONE VERSION OF THE CORRESPONDING NULL HYPOTHESIS:

There is no true relationship between social standing in campus organizations and gregariousness.

ANOTHER VERSION OF THE CORRESPONDING NULL HYPOTHESIS:

The relationship between social standing in campus organizations and gregariousness is nonexistent in the population from which the sample was drawn.

Example 3.7.2

RESEARCH HYPOTHESIS:

Private school graduates have a higher proportion of fathers in high-status occupations than public school graduates.

ONE VERSION OF THE CORRESPONDING NULL HYPOTHESIS:

There is no true difference in the proportion of fathers in high-status occupations between the populations of private school and public school graduates.

ANOTHER VERSION OF THE CORRESPONDING NULL HYPOTHESIS:

The observed difference between the proportions of fathers in high-status occupations for private school graduates and public school graduates is the result of chance variations associated with the random sampling process.

Exercise for Chapter 3

Because the application of many of the guidelines in this chapter involves a certain amount of subjectivity, there may be some legitimate differences of opinions on the best answers to some of the questions.

PART A: Answer the questions based on the guidelines presented in this chapter.

1. Is it permissible to include more than one hypothesis in a single sentence? Explain.

2. Very briefly explain why it is desirable to write a numbered (or lettered) list of hypotheses when more than one hypothesis will be examined in a single research study.

3. Why should the hypothesis or hypotheses be stated before the research methods are described?

4. Is the phrase "The hypothesis is…." *or* the phrase "The hypothesis was…." more appropriate in a research proposal?

5. Is the following sentence a hypothesis? Explain.

   "Based on the literature reviewed above, it was predicted that politicians who emphasize position XXX will be viewed more favorably by the electorate than politicians who emphasize position YYY."

6. Rewrite the following directional hypothesis to make it nondirectional.

   "Primary-grade students taught reading with the XYZ method will obtain higher reading comprehension test scores than those taught with the ABC method."

7. Write a null hypothesis that corresponds to the following research hypothesis.

   "It is hypothesized that there is a direct relationship between the extent to which social workers empathize with their clients and the clients' rate of compliance with the XYZ rule."

PART B

8. Write a directional hypothesis on a topic of interest to you. Then write a corresponding null hypothesis for it.

9. Rewrite the directional hypothesis that you wrote for Question 8 to make it nondirectional.

PART C

10. Review journal articles and/or theses or dissertations, and locate a statement that contains two or more hypotheses incorporated in a single sentence. Copy the statement, and bring it to class for discussion.

11. Review three journal articles and/or theses or dissertations that contain explicit statements of hypotheses, and make note of the following:
    a. In how many cases are the hypotheses stated in the last paragraph before the heading "Method"? (Note: In a thesis or dissertation, a hypothesis usually will be stated before the chapter on research methods.)
    b. In how many cases did the authors use alternative terms such as "predict" or "expect" instead of "hypothesize" in the statements of the hypotheses?
    c. How many of the hypotheses are directional, and how many are nondirectional? If both types are found, copy an example of each.
    d. How many of the statements of the hypotheses can be improved in some way? Explain.

12. If you will be writing a thesis or dissertation, examine theses or dissertations in your college/university library. Do any of them contain statements of the null hypothesis? If yes, copy one, and bring it to class for discussion.

Chapter 4

Writing Research Purposes, Objectives, and Questions

Often, researchers do not state hypotheses either because they are not interested in examining relationships between variables or because they believe that there is too little knowledge on a topic to permit formulation of hypotheses. Under these circumstances, a *research purpose* (also called a *research objective*) or a *research question* should be substituted for a hypothesis.

The principles for writing hypotheses should be followed when writing research purposes and questions. The following guidelines indicate when to state the latter instead of hypotheses and illustrate the application of some of the guidelines in Chapters 2 and 3 when writing purposes and questions.

➤ Guideline 4.1   If you will be conducting *qualitative* research, consider writing a research purpose or question instead of a hypothesis.

Many qualitative researchers approach their research topics without imposing hypotheses derived from theory or previous research. Nevertheless, they need to state a research purpose or question at the onset of their research, even if the purpose or question is quite general. Many qualitative researchers "follow the data." For example, during the course of a sequence of interviews, they may shift directions based on the early respondents' replies, change the nature of the questions for subsequent respondents, and, as a result, they might even modify their initial research purpose or question.

In *quantitative* research, research hypotheses, purposes, or questions also can be used. Note, however, that in such research, the specific research plans, including hypotheses, purposes, or questions, are very seldom modified during the course of the research.

➢ Guideline 4.2   When the goal of research is to describe one or more groups without describing relationships among variables, write a research purpose or question instead of a hypothesis.

As you recall from Chapter 2, a simple research hypothesis predicts a relationship between two variables. Note that in Example 4.2.1, no relationships are being examined. Instead, the researchers want to determine only one thing—the "level of public support." Hence, it would be inappropriate to try to state it as a hypothesis. A statement of the purpose is appropriate.

Example 4.2.1

Our purpose was to determine the level of public support for the bond issue for funding the construction of additional public libraries.

Likewise, no relationship is implied in Example 4.2.2. Instead, the researchers want to determine only what is being done to provide "practical training on ethical issues…."

Example 4.2.2

The purpose of our research was to determine what traditional graduate training programs in nursing were doing to provide practical training on ethical issues regarding euthanasia.

Notice that Examples 4.2.1 and 4.2.2 could have been stated as research questions, as illustrated in Example 4.2.3.

Example 4.2.3

What is the level of public support for the bond issue for funding the construction of additional public libraries?

What are traditional graduate training programs in nursing doing to provide practical training on ethical issues regarding euthanasia?

The choice between stating a research purpose or a research question is a matter of choosing the form that reads more smoothly in a particular context. One form is not inherently preferable to the other.

➢ Guideline 4.3   When there is insufficient evidence to permit formulation of a hypothesis regarding a relationship between variables, write a research purpose or question.

Prior to the terrorist attack on September 11, 2001, there had been no research on the psychological effects of terrorism of such great magnitude on children in the United States. In light of the lack of previous research, it would have been more appropriate after the attack to state a research question instead of a hypothesis, as is done in Example 4.3.1.

Example 4.3.1

Research Question: What was the nature and extent of the psychological impact of the terrorist attack of September 11, 2001, on middle-school children residing in the greater New York City metropolitan area?

Example 4.3.1 could be rewritten as a research purpose without changing the meaning of the author's question, as illustrated in Example 4.3.2.

Example 4.3.2

Research Purpose: To explore the nature and extent of the psychological impact of the terrorist attack of September 11, 2001, on middle-school children residing in the greater New York City metropolitan area.

➢ Guideline 4.4   When writing a research question, avoid writing a question that implies that the data will lead to a simple "yes" or "no" answer.

Example 4.4.1 violates this guideline. Most research is based on complex concepts, and the results are usually not simple. Yet Example 4.4.1 implies that the researchers are interested only in a "yes" or "no" answer. The improved version is a more interesting question, and the results will facilitate a comparison of the effectiveness of the new drug with existing ones.

Example 4.4.1

Research Question: Does the new drug (XXX) decrease blood pressure?

Improved Version of Example 4.4.1

Research Question: To what extent does the new drug (XXX) decrease blood pressure?

Compare Example 4.4.2 and its improved version. Research on complex human behavior such as reading comprehension seldom yields a simple "yes" or "no" answer.

Example 4.4.2

Research Question: In the long run, is a literature-based approach to teaching reading better than a phonics-based approach?

Improved Version of Example 4.4.2

Research Question: In the long run, what are the relative contributions of literature-based and phonics-based approaches to teaching reading?

Of course, the terms "long run," "literature-based approach," and "phonics-based approach" will need to be defined in the research report. We will consider definitions in Chapter 7 of this book.

➢ Guideline 4.5 The research purpose or question should be as specific as possible, yet stated concisely.

The need for specificity in hypotheses is discussed in Chapters 2 and 3. Application of this guideline to hypotheses, purposes, and questions is often more problematic than one might realize at first. Consider, for instance, Example 4.5.1. It is quite specific, actually naming two specific scales (i.e., measuring tools). However, for readers who are not familiar with the specific instruments (e.g., tests, questionnaires, and scales), the research purpose may be too specific.[1] Thus, writers must judge whether their audiences are likely to be familiar with the specific item(s) mentioned—in this case, the specific scales.

Example 4.5.1

The purpose was to determine the extent to which college students' scores on the Voloskovoy Self-Esteem Scale correlate with scores on the Smith-Doe Cultural Tolerance Inventory.

---

[1] Instruments such as attitude scales need to be described in detail in the section of the research report on methods. This topic is covered in Chapter 9.

For readers who are not familiar with the specific scale and inventory, the First Improved Version of Example 4.5.1 is superior. The Second Improved Version does not mention "scores" and "measure," yet the purpose is still clear. Since the Second Improved Version is stated more simply than the first, it is arguably better. Of course, readers of the research report will expect to learn later in the report how the two variables were measured.

First Improved Version of Example 4.5.1

The purpose was to determine the extent to which college students' scores on a measure of self-esteem correlate with scores on a measure of their tolerance of cultural differences.

Second Improved Version of Example 4.5.1

The purpose was to determine the extent to which college students' self-esteem correlates with their tolerance of cultural differences.

➢ Guideline 4.6   When stating related purposes or questions, consider presenting them in a numbered or lettered list.

In Example 4.6.1, the researchers present a numbered list of questions.

Example 4.6.1

1. How are mothers' perceptions of their parenting strengths different from the impressions reported by early adolescents about the same characteristics?
2. In the overall ratings of mothers, what are the prominent strengths identified by each generation?
3. What are the most important learning needs of mothers from both respondent groups?[2]

The numbered list in Example 4.6.1 allows the researchers to refer to individual research questions by number later in the report. For instance, in the results section, a researcher might say, "The results for Research Question 2 clearly indicate that...."

In Example 4.6.2, the researchers start with a general, overarching research question followed by a lettered list of the specific questions on

---

[2] Based on Strom et al. (2002, p. 398). For instructional purposes, some of the researchers' questions are omitted in this example.

which data were collected. This arrangement is usually desirable when there are a number of related research questions that were investigated.

Example 4.6.2

This study examined the following research question: How do community-dwelling adults communicate their end-of-life preferences to their significant others and to their health care providers? The more specific research questions included (a) With whom did they discuss their end-of-life preferences? (b) What prompted the discussions? (c) What do adults include as content in their end-of-life discussions? and (d) How did they carry out these discussions?[3]

➤ Guideline 4.7   In a research report, a research purpose or question should flow from the narrative that immediately precedes it.

Research reports typically begin with an introduction and literature review. These elements of a report should logically lead the reader to the research purposes or questions (or hypotheses). Example 4.7.1 shows the final two sentences of the last paragraph of an introduction that included a literature review on self-cutting (an increasingly popular form of self-mutilation, especially among adolescents). The research questions that follow the paragraph flow directly from it.

Example 4.7.1

Nevertheless, up to now, there has been no research in Hong Kong to study the self-cutting behavior of adolescents, especially the parental influence and response (Yip, 1998). …we conducted a qualitative study of parental influence on and response to adolescent self-cutting in Hong Kong.

Research Questions
There were three research questions in this study:
1. In what ways have the parents influenced their children's self-cutting?
2. How did the parents respond to their children's self-cutting?
3. How was the parent–child relationship affected by the self-cutting?[4]

---

[3] McDonald et al. (2003, p. 656).
[4] Yip, Ngan, & Lam (2003, p. 406).

Exercise for Chapter 4

PART A

1. For which of the following types of research would stating a research hypothesis be less likely?

   A. Quantitative research.   B. Qualitative research.

2. According to this chapter, is stating a research question inherently better than stating a research purpose?

3. Rewrite this research purpose as a research question: "The purpose of this research is to estimate the extent to which religious affiliation predicts voter sentiment regarding bond issues for public schools."

4. If a researcher wanted to poll hospital nurses only to determine if a majority favored a strike if a new labor contract was not agreed on by a specific date, would it be appropriate to state a research hypothesis? Explain.

5. Which of the guidelines in this chapter is clearly violated in the following research question?

   "Is the Internet useful for teaching geography?"

6. Which of the guidelines in this chapter is violated by the following research purpose?

   "The purpose is to determine whether the use of the Barnes Advocacy Teaching Method results in higher scores on the Dobrowsky Scale of International Understanding."

7. Which of the following arrangements is recommended in this chapter?

   A. Present a narrative introduction that flows from the research purpose or question that is stated first.

   B. Present a research purpose or question that flows from the narrative that immediately precedes it.

PART B

8. Write a research purpose on a topic of interest to you. Then rewrite it as a research question. Which form (i.e., purpose *or* question) do you prefer? Why?

PART C

9. Review three journal articles and/or theses or dissertations that contain statements of purposes or questions, and make note of the following:

   A. In how many cases are the purposes or questions presented in the last paragraph before the section on methods?

   B. In how many cases are the purposes or questions stated in the last sentence before the section on methods?

Chapter 5

Writing Titles

Because titles perform the important function of helping consumers of research identify research reports that are of interest to them, titles should be written with considerable care.

➢ Guideline 5.1   If only a small number of variables is studied, the title should name the variables.

In Example 5.1.1, there are two variables: (1) self-esteem and (2) aggressiveness.

Example 5.1.1
The Relationship Between Self-Esteem and Aggressiveness

Notice that the title in this example is not a complete sentence and does not end with a period mark, which are appropriate characteristics of titles.

➢ Guideline 5.2   If many variables are studied, only the *types* of variables should be named.

Suppose a researcher examined how students' attitudes toward school change over time with attention to differences among urban, suburban, and rural groups; various socioeconomic groups; girls and boys; and so on. Because there are too many variables to name in a concise title, only the main variable(s) needs to be specifically named; the others may be referred to by type, as illustrated in Example 5.2.1, where the main variable of "attitudes toward school" is mentioned, while the term "demographic variables" is used to stand for a variety of background variables such as socioeconomic status and gender.

Example 5.2.1

Relationships Between Students' Attitudes Toward School with Selected Demographic Variables

➢ Guideline 5.3   The title of a journal article should be concise; the title of a thesis or dissertation may be longer.

Titles of journal articles tend to be concise. A simple survey that we conducted illustrates this point. A count of the number of words in the titles of a random sample of 152 research articles on mathematics education that appeared in 42 journals in a recent year revealed that the median (average) number of words was close to 11. Example 5.3.1 is the shortest one identified in the survey; it is exceptionally short and could be improved by incorporating reference to the variables studied.

Example 5.3.1

The Mathematics Department

Example 5.3.2 is the longest one identified in the survey. It is long only because the specific countries are listed. If it ended with "in Various Countries" instead of the list, it would be more concise but less descriptive. If the research report was for dissemination in the United States, an alternative would be to end the title with "...in the United States and Other Countries."

Example 5.3.2

Grade Placement of Addition and Subtraction Topics in Japan, Mainland China, the Soviet Union, Taiwan, and the United States

Example 5.3.3 shows a title of about average length for the sample of titles examined. It illustrates Guideline 5.2; the *types* of variables, "personality factors" and "biographical factors," are referred to; the specific personality traits and types of biographical data collected are not spelled out.

Example 5.3.3

Contributions of Some Personality and Biographical Factors to Mathematical Creativity

For a random sample of titles of dissertations on mathematics education during the same recent year, the average number of words in the titles was almost 19, which is considerably more than the average of 11 for journal articles. A variation on the longest dissertation title is shown in Example 5.3.4.

Example 5.3.4

A Descriptive Study of Verbal Problems in Mathematics Textbooks for Grades Seven and Eight from Five Time Periods: The Late 70s, the Early 80s, the Late 80s, the Early 90s, and the Late 90s

Ask your instructor or chair of your thesis or dissertation committee whether they want you to write a concise title, such as those commonly used in journals, or a longer title, which is more typical (but not universal) in theses and dissertations. If a shorter title is desired, the shortened version shown immediately below could be used.

Shortened Version of the Title in Example 5.3.4

Verbal Problems in Mathematics Textbooks for Grades Seven and Eight from the Late 70s Through the Late 90s

➢ Guideline 5.4   A title should indicate what was studied —not the results or conclusions of the study.

All the previous examples illustrate this principle. Example 5.4.1 violates the principle; it is corrected in the improved version. Note that the researchers studied a large number of symptoms, which makes their improved version of the title more appropriate than the first version because the first version mentions only depression and muscle aches, which may mislead potential readers into assuming that these are the only symptoms studied.

Example 5.4.1

The Most Prevalent Symptoms of HIV-Infected Women are Severe Depression and Muscle Aches, Which Reduce the Quality of Life

Improved Version of Example 5.4.1

The Influence of Symptoms on Quality of Life Among HIV-Infected Women[1]

---

[1] Hudson, Kirksey, & Holzemer (2004, p. 9).

Guideline 5.4 may surprise some beginning students of empirical methods because results and conclusions are often stated in titles in the popular press. This is the case because the press frequently reports straightforward facts; "Five Die in Downtown Hotel Fire" is a perfectly acceptable title for a factual article of limited scope. Because empirical research reports are likely to raise as many questions as they resolve, a title that states a simple factual result or conclusion is usually inappropriate.

➢ Guideline 5.5   Consider mentioning the population(s) in a title when a study is deliberately delimited to a particular type of population.

In Example 5.5.1, the population is delimited to African American college students.

Example 5.5.1

Spirituality and Academic Performance Among African American College Students[2]

In Example 5.5.2, the title indicates that the population consists of ethnically diverse middle-school students. Such information helps consumers of research decide whether the research article will be of interest to them.

Example 5.5.2

Gender Labels and Gender Identity as Predictors of Drug Use Among Ethnically Diverse Middle School Students[3]

Note that sometimes a particular type of participant is studied only because that type is readily available to a researcher. For instance, a researcher might conduct a study on a theory of learning using students enrolled in his or her introductory psychology class (because they are readily available) even though the researcher is interested in the application of the theory to students in general. In such a case, mention of the type of population in the title is less important than when a researcher deliberately selects students enrolled in introductory psychology classes because their behavior is of particular interest in the research.

---

[2] Walker & Dixon (2002, p. 107).
[3] Kulis, Marsiglia, & Hecht (2002, p. 442).

➤ Guideline 5.6   Consider the use of subtitles to amplify the purposes or methods of study.

The following three examples illustrate this guideline.

Example 5.6.1

The Role of Alcoholism in Dysfunctional Families: A Pilot Study

Example 5.6.2

Kindergarten Teachers' Definitions of Literacy: A Survey of Experienced Teachers

Example 5.6.3

The Effects of Dynamic Therapy on Returning Soldiers: A Field Experiment

➤ Guideline 5.7   If a study is strongly tied to a particular model or theory, consider mentioning it in the title.

Some consumers of research are especially interested in studies that shed light on particular models or theories. If a study was designed to explore some aspect of these, mentioning this fact in the title will help consumers locate relevant research. The following two titles illustrate this guideline.

Example 5.7.1

The Role of Male Siblings in the Mathematics Achievement of Adolescent Girls: A Social Learning Theory Perspective

Example 5.7.2

Self-Control and Alcohol Restraint: An Initial Application of the Self-Control Strength Model[4]

➤ Guideline 5.8   A title may be in the form of a question; this form should be used sparingly and with caution.

Questions, when used as titles, are less formal than titles in the form of statements. Thus, questions as titles are sometimes preferred in less

---

[4] Muraven, Collins, & Nienhaus (2002, p. 113).

formal types of publications such as staff newsletters and workshop materials.

When using a question as a title for a research report, avoid stating it as a question that implies that it can be answered with a simple "yes" or "no." Notice that Example 5.8.1 implies that the result will be a simple "yes" or "no" answer, which is seldom the case in empirical research. Remember that empirical methods give us only varying degrees of confidence in results—not final answers. In the First Improved Version of Example 5.8.1, the problem has been fixed by posing the question in such a way that it cannot be answered with a simple "yes" or "no." The Second Improved Version of Example 5.8.1 shows that the problem can be avoided by *not* using the question form.

Example 5.8.1

Do Private Colleges and Universities Accommodate Students with Physical Disabilities?

First Improved Version of Example 5.8.1

To What Extent Do Private Colleges and Universities Accommodate Students with Physical Disabilities?

Second Improved Version of Example 5.8.1

The Accommodation of Students with Physical Disabilities by Private Colleges and Universities

➢ Guideline 5.9   In titles, use the words "effect" and "influence" with caution.

The words "effect" and "influence" are frequently used in the titles of research reports in which cause-and-effect relationships were studied. To examine such relationships, true experimental, quasi-experimental, or rigorous ex post facto methods should usually be employed. As a general rule, only reports on these methods should contain these words in their titles.

Examples 5.9.1 and 5.9.2 illustrate the typical use of the word "effect" in a title. The general form is: "The effect(s) of an independent variable (treatments or stimulus) on a dependent variable (outcome or response)."

Example 5.9.1

The Effects of Three Schedules of Reinforcement on the Maze Performance of Rats

Example 5.9.2

The Effects of Having Students Retell Stories in Writing on Their Achievement on a Standardized Test of Writing Skills

Note that "effect" is used as a noun in the two examples. As a noun, it means "influence." When used as a noun, the word "affect" means "feelings or emotions." Clearly, "effect" is the correct noun to use in these examples.

➢ Guideline 5.10   A title should be consistent with the research hypothesis, purpose, or question.

In Example 5.10.1, a research purpose is stated. The corresponding title closely mirrors the statement of the purpose.

Example 5.10.1

RESEARCH PURPOSE: Thus, the purpose of this study was to assess whether separate groups of exercisers, based on their resting heart rate, differed in scores on self-efficacy.

CORRESPONDING TITLE: Psychophysiological Comparison of Self-Efficacy and Resting Heart Rate[5]

In Example 5.10.2, the title refers to the variable named in the hypothesis.

Example 5.10.2

RESEARCH HYPOTHESIS: Specifically, we hypothesized that adolescents whose families had been in the United States for fewer generations would be more resistant to peer pressure than their counterparts whose families had been in the United States for more generations.

CORRESPONDING TITLE: Generational Differences in Resistance to Peer Pressure Among Mexican-Origin Adolescents[6]

---

[5] Wiggins (2002, p. 720).
[6] Umaña-Taylor & Bámaca-Gómez (2003, p. 183).

➤ Guideline 5.11 Consider mentioning unique features of a study in its title.

Suppose you conducted the first long-term follow-up study on the effects of a drug. You would be wise to indicate that your study is a long-term one in the title, as shown in Example 5.11.1.

Example 5.11.1

The Long-Term Effects of Tetracycline on Tooth Enamel Erosion

➤ Guideline 5.12 Avoid clever titles, especially if they fail to communicate important information about the report.

In Example 5.12.1, only "Publishing Criminal Justice Research" is informative. The reader will assume that an article deals with contemporary issues unless the title indicates that the study is historical; thus, reference to the new millennium is not needed. The subtitle is completely uninformative. It very vaguely refers to what is *not* covered—instead, it should specifically indicate what *is* presented in the report.

Example 5.12.1

Publishing Criminal Justice Research in the New Millennium: Things Gutenberg Never Taught You

In Example 5.12.2, the words "Taking the Sting Out of Stuttering" is a rhetorical phrase that does not contribute to our understanding of the topic of the research. The phrase should be omitted.

Example 5.12.2

Taking the Sting Out of Stuttering: A Comparison of the Effectiveness of Two Methods for Treating Stuttering

In general, throughout research reports, avoid the temptation to be clever or humorous. The function of a research report is to inform—not entertain.

Exercise for Chapter 5

PART A

1. When should only the *types* of variables studied be mentioned in a title?

2. Do the titles of journal articles tend to be longer than the titles of theses and dissertations?

3. Why should the title of a report of empirical research *not* state the results of a study?

4. According to this chapter, which are more formal as titles: statements *or* questions?

5. Which of the following titles is correct?

   A. The Affects of Treatment A on Outcome B
   B. The Effects of Treatment A on Outcome B

PART B: Comment on the adequacy of each of the following titles for research articles.

6. Registered Nurses Employed in Hospitals Report Higher Levels of Job Satisfaction When They Are Permitted to Participate in Decision Making

7. Watering the Proverbial Garden: Effective Communication Between Teachers and School Administrators

8. The Political Scientist

9. Are Age and Tenure Related to the Job Satisfaction of Social Workers?

10. Can Economists Predict Recessions?

11. The Effects of Peer Coaching on Achievement in English, Mathematics, History, Foreign Language, Geography, and Physics Among Tenth-, Eleventh-, and Twelfth-Graders: An Experiment Conducted in Five Major Urban Areas During the 2001–2002 School Year Using Multiple Measures of Achievement with Analyses by Gender and Grade Level

12. Forbidden Fruit Tastes Especially Sweet: A Study of Lawyers' Ethical Behavior

13. The Out-Migration from Southern California Is Driven by High Housing Costs

PART C: Write a title that you think would be appropriate for a research report that has this purpose: "The purpose of this research was to explore the effects of second-shift work schedules on psychological distress in young blue-collar families."

PART D: Name a purpose for research on a topic of interest to you, and write an appropriate title.

Chapter 6

Writing Introductions and Literature Reviews

The purpose of an introduction in an empirical research report is to introduce the problem area, establish its importance, and indicate the researcher's perspectives on the problem. Introductions usually conclude with an explicit statement of the research hypotheses, purposes, or questions explored in the study.

In a research report published as a journal article, the introduction is almost always integrated with the literature review into a single essay. In theses and dissertations, it is common to have the first chapter present the introduction and the second one present the literature review.

The guidelines that follow apply to all types of empirical research reports and proposals, except where noted.

➢ Guideline 6.1   Start the introduction by describing the problem area; gradually shift its focus to specific research hypotheses, purposes, or questions.

To implement the first guideline, write a topic outline of what will be covered. Example 6.1.1 shows a simple outline that starts with the broad topic and becomes more specific, ending with research purposes.

Example 6.1.1

Topic Outline for the Introduction

1. Importance of question asking by children
    a. As a skill used in learning in school
    b. As a functional skill in the home and other nonschool settings
2. Introduction to two types of questions
    a. Request for factual information (who, what, and when)
    b. Questions about causation (why)
    c. Functions of the two types in school
3. Relationship between parents' and children's verbal behavior

a. On other verbal variables
b. On question-asking behavior: quantity and type
4. Relationship between culture and verbal behavior
   a. Examples of how and why cultures may vary in their question-asking behavior
   b. Functions of questions in target cultures
5. Statement of the research purposes
   a. Determine types and numbers of questions asked by children in a structured learning environment
   b. Determine the relationship between question asking by children and by parents, with attention to both number and type
   c. Determine differences in question-asking behavior among target cultures

If this outline was for a thesis or dissertation, the author would write the introduction with an emphasis on his or her own views and observations regarding these topics with few citations of published literature. It would be appropriate to point out that the topics will be covered in more detail in the literature review, which is usually the second chapter.

If Example 6.1.1 was an outline for an introduction to a research report written to be published as a journal article, the literature review would be integrated with the author's introductory remarks.

If you are writing a research report as a term project, check with your instructor to see if you should write a separate introduction or one that is integrated with the literature review.

➢ Guideline 6.2   Start long introductions and literature reviews with a paragraph that describes their organization, and use subheadings to guide readers.

The numbered topics in Example 6.2.1 (e.g., *Importance of question asking by children* and *Introduction to two basic types of questions*) could be used as subheadings.

In theses and dissertations, where the introduction and literature review are usually each a fairly long chapter, the use of subheadings is especially desirable. Begin each chapter with an overview of what is covered in it, and begin each subsection with such an overview. This is illustrated in Example 6.2.1, in which the first paragraph provides an overview of the chapter, and the second paragraph provides an overview of the first subsection. The third paragraph then begins a discussion on the topic covered by the first subsection with citations to the literature (i.e., "Two major studies…").

Example 6.2.1

CHAPTER 2

LITERATURE REVIEW

This chapter describes literature relevant to the research purposes of this thesis. It is organized into four sections: (1) the importance of question asking by children, (2) an introduction to two basic types of questions, (3) the relationship between parents' and children's verbal behavior, and (4) the relationship between culture and verbal behavior. At the end of each section, the relevance of the literature to the research reported in this thesis is discussed.

Importance of Question Asking by Children

Most of the literature on the importance of question asking deals with the behavior of students in school settings during learning activities. This literature is reviewed first in order to establish the importance of question asking as a tool in the learning/teaching process. Then, the more limited literature on the importance of question asking by children as a functional skill in the home and other nonschool settings is reviewed. Throughout, there is an emphasis on the principles of learning theories as well as theories of social interaction that underlie the literature.

Two major studies examined the relationship between students' question-asking behavior and….

➢ Guideline 6.3   The importance of a topic should be explicitly stated in the introduction.

Be specific in giving reasons for the importance of the topic, as illustrated in Example 6.3.1, which is the beginning of the first paragraph in the introduction to a research report.

Example 6.3.1

Poor eating habits and inactive lifestyles that begin during childhood can lead to numerous health problems, including obesity, diabetes, heart disease and cancer (U.S. Department of Health and Human Services, 1997). Only one in five children eat five servings of fruit and vegetables a day as recommended by the National Cancer Institute to reduce cancer risk later in life (Krebs-Smith et al., 1996). In addition….[1]

---

[1] Bauer, Yang, & Austin (2004, p. 34).

➤ Guideline 6.4   A statement on the importance of a topic should be specific to the topic investigated.

Example 6.4.1 was submitted as the statement on the importance of a topic in the first draft of a proposal for a thesis in which a functional skills program in adult schools was to be evaluated. Notice that the statement fails to deal specifically with functional skills in adult education. In fact, the statement is so broad that it could refer to almost any curriculum and instruction topic in education, which is clearly a violation of the guideline.

Example 6.4.1

Human resource is one of the greatest resources of this country, and education plays a major role in maintaining, nurturing, and protecting that resource. Thus, it is imperative that we find, evaluate, and utilize educational systems that yield the results necessary for the country's progress.

➤ Guideline 6.5   Consider pointing out the number or percentage of people who are affected by the problem you are studying.

Being able to show that many people are affected by a problem helps to establish the importance of a research problem (see Guidelines 6.3 and 6.4). Of course, the numbers and percentages should be specific—not just stated in the form of nonspecific generalizations such as "A large percentage of high school students report that…" or "An increasing number of people have…."

The authors of Examples 6.5.1 and 6.5.2 followed this guideline.

Example 6.5.1

Depression is one of the most frequently diagnosed psychiatric disorders in youth, with as many as 9% of children having experienced at least one episode of …major depression by the age of 14 (Lewinsohn, Rohde, Seeley, & Fischer, 1993). Prevalence rates for subsyndromal depressive symptoms are even greater, with between 10% and 30% of youth exceeding cutoff scores on self-report measures of depressive symptoms (Hammen & Rudolph, 2003) and between 20% and 59% of youth experiencing….[2]

---

[2] Abela & Sullivan (2003, p. 384).

Example 6.5.2

Attention Deficit Hyperactivity Disorder (ADHD) has become the most widely diagnosed psychiatric condition among children in the United States. Estimates of the percentage of children with ADHD vary from study to study, ranging from two to nine percent, but is generally accepted to affect five percent of the population of children under age 18 (Taylor, 1997).[3]

➤ Guideline 6.6   The literature review should be presented in the form of an essay—not in the form of an annotated list.

An annotation is a brief summary; a list of annotations indicates what research is available on a topic but fails to organize the material for the reader by indicating how the individual citations relate to one another and what trends the researcher has observed in the published literature on his or her topic.

An effective review of literature is an essay based on a *topic outline* (see Guideline 6.1) that takes the reader from topic to topic. The literature on a topic is cited during a discussion of that topic. Research reports with similar findings or methodologies may be cited together, as in Example 6.6.1. Notice that the first point is supported by two references while the last point (i.e., "girls tend to have…higher levels of depressive symptoms than do boys") is supported by three sources in the literature.

Example 6.6.1

Thus, adolescents who are dissatisfied with their body or physical appearance tend to report more depressive symptoms (Baron & Joly, 1988; Brooks-Gunn & Warren, 1989). The body image-depressed mood relationship seems to exist in both girls and boys (Lewinsohn, Roberts, Seeley, Rohole, Gotlieb, & Hops, 1994), but since girls tend to have a more negative body image, they also (on average) report higher levels of depressive symptoms than do boys (Allgood-Merten et al., 1990; Andrews et al., 1993; Mori & Morey, 1991).[4]

Example 6.6.2 also illustrates this guideline. Notice that the excerpt is organized around topics—not the findings of individual researchers. In fact, two of the references (i.e., Chang, 1997, and Weisner & Schmidt, 1992) are each cited two times—in support of two different points the author makes in the paragraph.

---

[3] Glass (2001, p. 70).
[4] Holsen, Kraft, & Røysamb (2001, p. 615).

Example 6.6.2

Epidemiological studies indicate that alcohol abuse and dependence occur about twice as often among men as among women (Chang, 1997; Weisner & Schmidt, 1992). However, women are underrepresented among individuals entering treatment for alcohol abuse, dependency, and related problems (Beckman, 1994; Dawson, 1996). Although there is some indication that the underutilization of alcohol treatment by women is changing, men have persistently outnumbered women in treatment by a ratio of almost 4:1 (Chang; Weisner & Schmidt). Among individuals in treatment for alcoholism, the proportion of women increased from 22 percent in 1982 to 29 percent in 1993 (U.S. Department of Health and Human Services [DHHS], 1997). This coincided with a similar national increase in specialized treatment services for women (DHHS).[5]

➤ Guideline 6.7   Avoid using long strings of reference citations for a single finding or theory.

Some findings or theories have been very widely reported in the literature. Suppose, for instance, that you found 32 journal articles that reported data that support the XYZ theory. It would be distracting as well as unproductive to make a simple statement to this effect followed by 32 reference citations in parentheses. One solution is to simply use "e.g.," standing for "for example," and cite only a few, as illustrated in Example 6.7.1.

Example 6.7.1

More than 30 experiments reported in journal articles have lent support to the XYZ theory (e.g., Doe, 2003; Smith & Smith, 2004; and Jones, 2005).

Another solution is to indicate the time span over which the support has been reported while citing only some of the early and some of the more recent experiments, as in Example 6.7.2.

Example 6.7.2

More than 30 experiments reported in journal articles have lent support to the XYZ theory, starting with studies conducted more than 50 years ago (e.g., Black, 1949; Barnes, 1950) and continuing to the present (Smith & Smith, 2004; Jones, 2005).

Still another solution is to cite only those that are strongest in terms of research methodology, as in Example 6.7.3.

---

[5] Parks, Hesselbrock, Hesselbrock, & Segal (2003, p. 151).

Example 6.7.3

More than 30 experiments reported in journal articles have lent support to the XYZ theory. Among these, three used true experimental designs with random assignment to treatment groups (Tanner, 2001; Clive, 2003; Banner & Brown, 2005).

Yet another solution is to distinguish among the reports based on the strength of their support, as in Example 6.7.4.

Example 6.7.4

More than 30 experiments reported in journal articles have lent support to the XYZ theory. While the support is weak in about half the studies (e.g., Green, 2004; Blake, 2005), stronger support has been reported in the others (e.g., White, 2001; Shoemaker, 2002).

In a thesis or dissertation, you may be expected to cite all relevant references to demonstrate that you have conducted a comprehensive literature search. Even in this circumstance, long strings of citations can be avoided by referring to the references in smaller groups. For instance, you can cite the methodologically strong ones in one place in the literature review, cite the older ones for a historical perspective in another place, cite the ones that led to turning points in thought on the issue in yet another place, and so on.

➤ Guideline 6.8   Discuss theories that have relevance to the research.

A theory is a cohesive set of principles that help explain relationships among variables. Pointing out how the research relates to one or more theories helps to establish the context for the research and helps to establish its importance. Discussion of theories can be integrated throughout the introduction and literature review, as indicated by this statement from Example 6.2.1 in this chapter: "Throughout, there is an emphasis on the principles of learning theories as well as theories of social interaction that underlie the literature." If there is an extended discussion of one or more related theories, it is also appropriate to discuss them in a separate section of the literature review with a subheading such as "Theoretical Rationale" or with a subheading that names the theory such as "Attachment Theory" in Example 1.5.2 in Chapter 1.

➢ Guideline 6.9 The literature review should emphasize the findings of previous research—not just the research methodologies and names of variables studied.

Example 6.9.1 violates this guideline. In the improved version, the major finding is summarized (i.e., respect for authority *declined* after the imposition of censorship).

Example 6.9.1

Doe (2003) studied respect for authority and how it changed after the imposition of censorship. This study is important because, being based on a two-year case study, it is the most intensive study to date of the effects of censorship on college students.

Improved Version of Example 6.9.1

Doe (2003) found that respect for authority among this group declined significantly after the imposition of censorship. This study is important because, being based on a two-year case study, it is the most intensive study to date of the effects of censorship on college students.

➢ Guideline 6.10 Feel free to express opinions about the quality and importance of the research being cited.

If a study is especially strong methodologically, consider mentioning it, as was done in the last sentence of the Improved Version of Example 6.9.1 above.

When there are contradictory findings among the studies on the research topic, give more weight to strong studies than to seriously flawed studies when reaching generalizations about the results of previous research.

Readers will assume that the research being cited is reasonably sound unless the writer states otherwise. Thus, it is desirable to point out major weaknesses in previous studies, as is illustrated in Example 6.10.1.

Example 6.10.1

Another commonly used method for assessing helping skills [of professionals such as counselors] has been to have judges code verbal response modes (e.g., reflection of feelings, interpretation) in transcripts of sessions (see Hill & Corbett, 1993). Although this coding method is adequate for assessing what helpers overtly do in sessions, it does not capture how clients perceive the skills.

A helper may deliver an interpretation, but the client may not hear it because she or he is distracted. What the client hears is undoubtedly more important than what judges code objectively.[6]

Note that it is not always necessary to discuss weaknesses in detail. Sometimes, it is sufficient to tip off readers to weaknesses with short phrases such as "In a preliminary pilot study, Doe (2004) found...." and "Although the researchers did not use random assignment to experimental and control groups, the study by Jones and Black (2005) is...."

➢ Guideline 6.11   Point out trends and themes in the literature.

In Example 6.11.1, the researcher points out a recent trend in the literature.

Example 6.11.1

A recent trend in the literature is the self-reflection of White teachers who teach in predominantly African American settings. These teachers admit to having to shift their attitudes about teaching and learning to obtain acceptable achievement outcomes (Diller, 1999; Kottler, 1997; Weiner, 1999). Traditional teaching methods often failed to yield desirable outcomes in these teachers' classrooms. Success in the classroom came only after a shift in their attitudes about teaching, learning and culture. Shifts in attitudes of these teachers involve viewing culture as a tool in teaching rather than ignoring it.[7]

➢ Guideline 6.12   Point out gaps in the literature.

In Example 6.12.1, the researchers point out gaps in the literature on the role of religion in the lives of young people.

Example 6.12.1

Although previous investigations provide some insight into these [research] questions [stated immediately above], research in this area generally...focuses on young adults (i.e., college students) rather than on early, middle, or late adolescents...[and] its findings are based on samples that are often small...[and] limited to a single location....[8]

---

[6] Hill & Kellems (2002, p. 264).
[7] Bakari (2003, p. 641).
[8] Wallace, Forman, Caldwell, & Willis (2003, pp. 103–104).

In Example 6.12.2, the gap in the literature is referred to as a "limitation" of the body of research on the topic.

Example 6.12.2

One final limitation of most prior studies of maternal teaching interactions is that they have neglected children's contributions to the learning environment. The simple framework of most of the literature on parental teaching is that mothers teach and children learn. Yet children, too, contribute to the learning environment through their use of questions and their own discussion of complex ideas.[9]

Students who are writing term project papers, theses, and dissertations should note that when they point out gaps in the literature, they may be asked by their professors to defend such assertions. Thus, it is a good idea to keep careful records of how the literature search was conducted (i.e., what indices and databases were examined—including the dates) and which descriptors (i.e., subject index terms) were used in the search. Students should consider including a statement such as the one in Example 6.12.3 in their reports; such statements are usually *not* included in research reports published in journals.

Example 6.12.3

A search of the ABC Index for the years 1975 through 2005 using the subject index terms "term a" and "term b" yielded only two studies of adolescents (i.e., Doe, 2003; Jones, 2005) and no studies of children.

➤ Guideline 6.13 Point out how the current study differs from previous studies.

Unless you are conducting a strict replication of a previous study, you should point out how your study differs from previously published research. The differences may be in terms of your selection of variables, how you conceptualized and measured the variables, the composition of the sample, the method of analysis, and so on. After showing that the literature supports the generalization that violence in TV programming reduces memory of the associated commercials, the authors of Example 6.13.1 point out how their study differs from the previous ones.

---

[9] Eisenberg (2002, p. 210).

Example 6.13.1

However, we could find no published studies on the effect of televised sex on memory for commercial messages. The main purpose of the current study is to examine whether sexual content in TV programming reduces memory for commercials in the same way that violent programming does.[10]

➤ Guideline 6.14   Peripheral research may be cited in a thesis or dissertation when no literature with a direct bearing on the research topic can be located.

When Los Angeles first started implementing year-round school schedules, for example, there was no published research on the topic. There was research, however, on traditional school-year programs in which children attended school in shifts, on the effects of the length of the school year on achievement, and on the effectiveness of summer school programs. Students who were writing theses and dissertations on the Los Angeles program had to cite such peripheral literature in order to demonstrate their ability to conduct a search of the literature and write a comprehensive, well-organized review of literature. Remember that a thesis or dissertation is, in part, a test of a student's ability to locate, collect, and integrate references into a cohesive essay.

In a research report published as a journal article, it would probably suffice to say that a systematic search of the literature revealed no studies on this topic.

➤ Guideline 6.15   Use direct quotations sparingly in literature reviews.

This guideline is suggested for three reasons. First, direct quotations often do not convey their full meaning when quoted out of context; on the other hand, quoting the context is usually less efficient than paraphrasing the main idea(s) of the author. Second, frequent quotations may disrupt the flow of the review because of the varying writing styles of the authors. Finally, quotations often bog the reader down in details that are not essential for the purpose of obtaining an overview of the literature. By paraphrasing, you can easily omit minor details.

---

[10] Bushman & Bonacci (2002, p. 558).

Direct quotations are appropriate when the writer of the review (1) wants to illustrate either the original author's skill at writing or lack thereof or (2) believes that the wording of a statement will have an emotional impact on the reader that would be lost in paraphrase. These purposes seldom arise in presenting literature in an empirical research report.

➤ Guideline 6.16   Report sparingly on the details of the literature being cited.

Because the research being cited has usually been published, the reader can obtain copies to learn the details.

Typically, reviews of literature in theses and dissertations contain more details on cited research than reviews in research reports published as journal articles. Even in theses and dissertations, however, the researcher should be selective in reporting details. For example, it may be appropriate to describe an especially important study in more detail than other, less important studies. Also, if your study builds directly on a previous study, it would be appropriate to discuss that study in detail so your readers can see the connection between them.

➤ Guideline 6.17   Consider using literature to provide the historical context for the present study.

Following this guideline is especially desirable in theses and dissertations where students should demonstrate that they have a comprehensive knowledge of the literature on their topics. It is also appropriate in research reports published as journal articles when researchers wish to (1) acknowledge the original proponents' theories and principles that underlie their current studies or (2) show that their research is a logical continuation of the historical chain of thought on a topic. Example 6.17.1 shows how the history of a topic might be briefly traced. In this example, the researchers trace the history of graphology, which claims that personality traits are revealed by handwriting characteristics. Example 6.17.2 traces the history of Attention Deficit Hyperactivity Disorder (ADHD).

Example 6.17.1

The rules on the method of classification of the system of [graphological] signs used today were laid down by Jean Crepieux-Jamin in his book…published in 1888. Authors of graphology texts intended both for the serious student (e.g., Singer, 1986; Nezes, 1993) and the populist market (e.g., Branstson, 1995) do indeed claim that indicators of personality traits or types of intellectual ability can be so identified. Supporting evidence from studies that used conventional, scientific methodology is, however, relatively rare or limited (Klimoski & Rafaeli, 1983; Beyerstein, 1992; Klimoski, 1992)…. Within the last 15 years or so, a number of controlled experiments have been reported in the (English language) academic press. These have generally involved attempts to match handwriting characteristics with other measures of personality….[11]

Example 6.17.2

ADHD has gone through a series of names since it was first documented in 1845, including (but not limited to) "restlessness syndrome," "minimal brain dysfunction," and "hyperkinetic reaction disorder" (Eisenberg & Esser, 1997; Moghadam & Fagan, 1994). However, in those earlier years, children who displayed the behaviors that are now commonly known as "ADHD" were often viewed as trouble-making, lazy, or disobedient children. In the 1970s, researchers began to more closely study these behaviors. As this research progressed during the following two decades, ADHD came to be viewed as a medical disorder….[12]

➤ Guideline 6.18   Consider citing prior literature reviews on your topic.

If there is a solid previous review of literature on your topic, consider citing it. Typically, you should describe the conclusions of the previous reviewer and indicate whether your reading of the literature has led you to the same conclusions. If so, it will lend support to your conclusions. If not, you should describe why you think the previous reviewer was led astray.

Of course, you will want to read the literature cited by the previous reviewer and present it in your own words. Finally, you will want to bring your readers up-to-date by discussing the literature published since the review you are citing was published.

---

[11] Lowis & Mooney (2001, pp. 367–368).
[12] Glass (2001, pp. 70–71).

➢ Guideline 6.19   When using the Harvard method for citing references, decide whether to emphasize the authorship or the content of each reference.

Note that in the Harvard method for citing references (also known as the "author–date method" popularized by the American Psychological Association), only the authors' last names and year of publication are given. The names may be made part of the sentence, as in Example 6.19.1, or they may be included parenthetically, as in Example 6.19.2. In Example 6.19.1, the emphasis is on the authorship; in Example 6.19.2, the emphasis is on the content or idea being expressed. The choice of forms depends on the desired emphasis. Because a literature review should be an essay that integrates and evaluates the content of previous research on a topic, presenting the researcher's name in parentheses, as in Example 6.19.2, is usually preferable because it deemphasizes the authorship.

Example 6.19.1

Doe (2004) reported that a major source of dissatisfaction among teachers appears to be the low social status accorded their profession.

Example 6.19.2

A major source of dissatisfaction among teachers appears to be the low social status accorded their profession (Doe, 2004).

➢ Guideline 6.20   Avoid referring to the credentials and affiliations of the authors of the literature that is reviewed.

In an "appeal to authority," writers in the popular press often refer to a researcher's credentials (e.g., being a professor) and affiliations (e.g., Harvard University) when summarizing research. Thus, in a newspaper article on recently released research, it would not be uncommon to see a statement such as "Professor Doe of Harvard University's School of Public Health reported in an article published today in the *Journal of Studies* that...." Such a statement in a formal academic report of empirical research should almost never be used because confidence in the results of a research study should rest on the strength of the evidence presented (in light of the care with which empirical methods were used in the research)—not in terms of the credentials or affiliations of the researchers.

➤ Guideline 6.21   Use of the first person is acceptable if used sparingly to refer to personal observations, experiences, and beliefs.

Use of the first person is especially appropriate when referring to the author's personal observations, experiences, and beliefs, as is the case in Example 6.21.1. The use of "I" in this example is less stilted than using the term "the author" to refer to the writer.

Example 6.21.1

I began to speculate on the origins of this problem during my three years as an assistant to a teacher of the learning disabled.

Frequent use of the first person throughout the introduction and elsewhere in a research report, however, can be distracting. It is especially inappropriate when referring to matters that are not personal such as the lack of experimental studies mentioned in Example 6.21.2.

Example 6.21.2

When I realized that all the previous research on this topic was nonexperimental, I decided that it would be especially important for me to conduct an experimental study for the current investigation.

Improved Version of Example 6.21.2

Because all the previous research on this topic was nonexperimental, it seemed especially important to conduct an experimental study for the current investigation.

Concluding Comments

For many students, writing the introduction and review of literature is the most difficult part of writing an empirical research report. The guidelines in this chapter will help you avoid some major pitfalls. They do not, however, cover other important matters in effective writing such as providing clear transitions and writing with a sparse but clear style. The latter can be mastered only through guided learning under the tutelage of an experienced writer and through extensive reading of effective prose.

If you lack confidence in your ability to write introductions and literature reviews, follow these suggestions:

1. Write a topic outline, as illustrated in Guideline 6.1, and take it with you when you consult with your instructor or committee. The outline will help them understand what you are trying to accomplish and make it easier for them to help you.
2. Read numerous reviews of literature, paying attention to how they are organized and how the authors make transitions from one topic to another.
3. After writing a first draft, have it reviewed by friends and colleagues— even if they are not experts on your topic. Ask them to point out elements that are not clear. Effective introductions are usually comprehensible to any intelligent layperson.
4. Be prepared to revise and rewrite. Because effective writing is achieved through this process, expect your instructor, committee, or journal editor to request revisions.

Exercise for Chapter 6

Because the application of many of the guidelines in this chapter involves a certain amount of subjectivity, there may be some legitimate differences of opinions on the best answers to some of the following questions.

PART A

1. According to this chapter, should the introduction/literature review begin with a statement of hypotheses/purposes/questions? Explain.

2. It is suggested that long introductions and literature reviews begin with what?

3. Critique the following paragraph, which was submitted by a student to indicate the importance of the topic she selected for her research (i.e., the prevalence of depression among inner-city adolescents).

    In the new millennium, the public is increasingly aware of the importance of the psychological well-being of all citizens. Because of this recognition by the public, it is important to conduct more studies that shed light on the prevalence of well-being, starting with the psychological well-being of adolescents, who will soon be adults.

4. Critique the following portions of a literature review.

> Smith (2002) conducted a national survey of women's attitudes toward national politically liberal policy issues. He found that....
>
> Jones (2004) also studied the tendency (on average) for women to hold more liberal positions on....
>
> Doe (2005) conducted an experiment in which college women were....

5. Critique the following description of the research by Jones. For instructional purposes, assume that the description is complete (i.e., other information about Jones' research is not described elsewhere in the research report).

> Jones (2003) conducted an experiment in which one random half of a group of college men attended a lecture on sexual harassment issues in the workplace. During the lecture, the lecturer told a mildly misogynous joke. The other random half heard the same lecture but was not told the joke. Immediately afterwards, all the men were administered a scale that measured their attitudes toward laws designed to protect women in employment settings. This is an important study since it utilized random assignment to treatments.

6. According to this chapter, what might readers assume if you cite literature without commenting on weaknesses in it?

7. How could the following beginning of the introduction to a research report be improved?

> In recent years, homelessness has been dramatically increasing. Now, large numbers of individuals are living on the streets in major American cities. Due to financial constraints, many social service organizations are unable to keep up with the demand for....

8. Suppose you located reports on 24 studies that indicated that X is larger than Y. According to this chapter, is it sufficient to make a statement to that effect followed by the 24 reference citations in parentheses? If no, what should be done?

9. A student wrote a literature review with a large number of quotations from the literature in the belief that the quotations would substantiate the points being made. According to this chapter, is this appropriate?

10. In the following statement from a literature review, the writer is critical of the research being cited. According to this chapter, is this acceptable?

The findings by Smith (2004) on the prevalence of substance abuse by middle-school students are highly questionable because she failed to collect the data anonymously.

11. "According to this chapter, it is appropriate to cite only recently published studies in a literature review." Is this statement true *or* false? Explain the basis for your answer.

12. Critique the following statement from a literature review.

    Dr. Richard Doe (2004), professor of education at Stanford University and former head of research for the New York Public Schools, reported on the effects of variable schedules of reinforcement on the mathematics achievement of....

13. Is the use of the first person (e.g., "I" and "me") ever acceptable in an introduction to a research report? Explain.

PART B

14. Examine the introductions to three research reports published in journals and/or theses or dissertations on a topic of interest to you, and answer the following questions.

    a. How many are organized according to Guideline 6.1?

    b. In how many does the author explicitly state why the research topic is important and cite specific numbers or percentages to support the statement? If any, copy one statement, and bring it to class for discussion.

    c. In how many does the author cite references to relevant theories? If any, what are the names of the theories? Are the discussions of the theories brief or in-depth?

    d. In how many is the literature review integrated with the introduction?

    e. In how many does the author express opinions on the quality of some of the research cited? If any, copy an example, and bring it to class for discussion.

    f. In how many cases are direct quotations from the literature included?

PART C: Write a topic outline for an introduction to a research project of interest to you. Have it reviewed by two friends or colleagues, and revise it in light of their comments. Bring the first and second drafts to class for discussion.

Notes:

Chapter 7

Writing Definitions

Two types of definitions are usually found in empirical research reports. Conceptual definitions, which resemble dictionary definitions that refer to general concepts, are often presented in the introduction. Operational definitions, which define traits in concrete, step-by-step physical terms, are usually presented in the section on methods.

In theses and dissertations, conceptual definitions are sometimes provided in a separate section of the introduction, with its own subheading. In journal articles, conceptual definitions are usually integrated into the introductory statement.

This chapter presents guidelines on what to define and how to write both conceptual and operational definitions.

➤ Guideline 7.1   All variables in a research hypothesis, purpose, or question should be defined.

Example 7.1.1 is a hypothesis. "Newspaper reading habits" and "cultural literacy" need to be defined in the research report.

Example 7.1.1

There is a direct relationship between newspaper reading habits and cultural literacy.

"Newspaper reading habits," for instance, can be defined in a number of ways. At the conceptual level, it might be generally defined in terms of "regularity of referring to newspapers for information and entertainment." At the operational (i.e., physical) level, the definition might refer to daily average number of minutes spent reading, the typical number of newspaper sections scanned, number of newspaper stories read, and so on. Obviously, how newspaper reading habits are defined at the operational level could have an important influence on the results of the study.

➢ Guideline 7.2   The definitions of defining attributes of a population (also called "control variables") should be specific.

In the hypothesis in Example 7.2.1, "adult education learners" is a defining attribute that should be specifically defined.

Example 7.2.1

There is a direct relationship between newspaper reading habits and cultural literacy among adult education learners.

The definition of "adult education learners" in Example 7.2.2 is not sufficiently specific. The improved version contains more details that help readers understand the characteristics of the population.

Example 7.2.2

"Adult education learners" are adults enrolled in formal education programs.

Improved Version of Example 7.2.2

"Adult education learners" are individuals over 18 years of age who are enrolled in one or more classes in adult schools operated by the Los Angeles Unified School District.

➢ Guideline 7.3   Theories and models on which the research is based should be defined.

The "stress–coping theory" mentioned in Example 7.3.1 should be defined. Notice that the researchers provide a reference where more information on the theory can be found.

Example 7.3.1

In the introduction to a research report, researchers state:

The stress–coping theory of addictive behaviors (Wills & Shiffman, 1985) has been successfully applied to alcohol abuse and has the potential to increase understanding of gambling.[1]

Then the researchers who wrote Example 7.3.1 devote seven paragraphs to fleshing out the definition of this theory as well as the definitions of

---

[1] Lightsey & Hulsey (2002, p. 202).

these two psychological constructs that underlie the theory: "stress" and "coping." For instance, they define a particular type of coping in Example 7.3.2. Notice the use of an example in parentheses to help readers understand the definition.

Example 7.3.2

Escape-avoidance coping consists of avoiding a stressful situation by engaging in a task not related to the stressor (e.g., drinking alcohol instead of interacting with the family).[2]

➢ Guideline 7.4   Conceptual definitions should be specific.

The definition of "*imitation*" in Example 7.4.1 is not sufficiently specific. In the improved version, much more information regarding the conceptual meaning of the term is provided. Note that it is perfectly acceptable to cite a definition previously offered by an expert (in this case, Wyrwicka, 1996). In fact, this is often preferable to trying to devise a new way to define a concept that already has a widely accepted definition.

Example 7.4.1

Imitation is the process of one person copying the behavior of another.

Improved Version of Example 7.4.1

Imitation is a particular activity that involves both social and cognitive dimensions and can be defined generally as "the copying by an individual of a certain motor or vocal act performed by another individual, usually of the same species" (Wyrwicka, 1996, p. 1). The findings of social learning show that the behavioral repertoire of infants can be modeled *by seeing the actions of others* (Bandura, 1997). Imitation occurs from birth (Meltzoff & Moore, 1977, 1997) and is an important functional basis for human development, including gestures, vocalizations, object manipulation, and tool using, as well as motor–social expressions, etc.[3]

---

[2] Lightsey & Hulsey (2002, p. 202).
[3] Toselli, Farneti, & Grossi (2001, p. 524).

➢ Guideline 7.5   Operational definitions should be provided, usually in the method section of a report.

An operational definition is one that is stated in terms of physical steps. After reading an operational definition, the reader should be able to see in his or her mind's eye the physical operations that were used to measure a variable, give treatments, define a population, or identify the relevant aspects of a model or theory.

In a study of anticipation strategies used on the first day of smoking cessation, the researchers who wrote Example 7.5.1 refer to specific physical behaviors—an essential characteristic of operational definitions.

Example 7.5.1

Stimulus control strategies include getting rid of all cigarettes and other smoking paraphernalia such as ashtrays and lighters and avoiding situations in which one usually smokes. *Symptom prevention strategies* include using nicotine replacement therapy (NRT) to decrease or prevent urges and withdrawal symptoms. *Social support strategies* involve telling others you are quitting in order to garner their help or understanding.[4]

Example 7.5.2 is not operational because it does not describe the specific physical actions taken in the presence of the participants in the experiment. This flaw has been corrected in the improved version.

Example 7.5.2

The stress-producing condition for the experimental group was a mild verbal threat given by the experimenter.

Improved Version of Example 7.5.2

In order to produce the stress-producing condition for the experimental group, a male experimenter dressed in a white doctor's jacket seated the participants. He introduced himself as a physician with a specialty in internal medicine and stated that for the purposes of the experiment, "You will receive a mild electric shock while we measure your blood pressure."

---

[4] O'Connell, Gerkovich, Bott, Cook, & Shiffman (2002, p. 150).

➤ Guideline 7.6   For each conceptual definition, there should be a corresponding operational definition.

For each conceptual definition in the introduction, there should be an operational definition, usually in the method section. Example 7.6.1 illustrates this guideline.

Example 7.6.1

Conceptual definition in the introduction:

Ainsworth (1989)...and others (e.g., Sroufe & Waters, 1977) defined attachment as a meaningful and enduring emotional bond between two people. The secure attachment relationship was thought to provide the child with a sense of security, comfort, and predictability. Such a bond would be an important resource for children charting new developmental terrain.

Corresponding operational definition in the method section:

ATTACHMENT TO PARENTS. The Parental Bonding Instrument (PBI; Parker, Tupling, & Brown, 1979) is a 50-item self-report questionnaire, with 25 items assessing relations with one's mother and the same 25 items assessing relations with one's father.... Participants are instructed to recall their impressions of their parents, as formed during the first 16 years of their lives, and then to respond to items that reflect these impressions on a 4-point scale ranging from *very like my mother/father* (1) to *very unlike my mother/father* (4). Two dimensions of parent–child attachment are assessed by the PBI: care and protection.[5]

Notice that the authors of Example 7.6.1 have operationalized "attachment" by describing a published questionnaire used to measure the variable "attachment to parents." This possibility is discussed under the next guideline.

A conceptual definition of a "hate crime" and a corresponding operational definition are provided in Example 7.6.2.

Example 7.6.2

Conceptual definition in the introduction:

Bias is a preformed negative attitude toward a group based on race, religion, ethnicity/national origin, sexual orientation, or disability status. A *bias crime*, also known as a *hate crime*, is a criminal offense committed against person or property that is motivated, in whole or in part, by the offender's bias.

Corresponding operational definition in the method section:

It is acknowledged that some hate crimes reported to law enforcement were not reported to [the FBI] and that other hate crimes were not reported to any local

---

[5] Rice, Cunningham, & Young (1997, p. 91).

law enforcement agency. However, data used in this analysis represented the complete universe of hate crimes *that have been properly reported to the FBI* as required by the Hate Crimes Statistics Act.[6]

Notice that the conceptual definition in Example 7.6.2 allows for hate crimes to be operationally defined in many ways such as surveying individuals to see if they believe they have been the victims of hate crimes. In contrast, the operational definition in the example is sufficiently specific that it rules out alternative methods of defining the variable. Also, note that reporting crimes to the FBI as well as obtaining the data from the FBI are physical acts that operationalize the variable.

➢ Guideline 7.7   If a published instrument was used, the variable measured by it may be operationally defined by citing the reference for the instrument.

A published instrument, such as an achievement test, almost always comes with specific, step-by-step physical directions for its use. By citing the test with a reference to the author and publisher of the test, a researcher can provide an operational definition. Example 7.7.1 provides such a definition.

Example 7.7.1

Beginning mathematics skill was defined as the composite score on Form S of the Primary Level 2, multiple-choice/open-ended Mathematics Test of the Stanford Achievement Test Series, Ninth Edition (Harcourt Brace, 2002).

To further operationalize the definition in Example 7.7.1, the author could provide an overview of the physical properties of the test (e.g., content of the items, number of items, types of items such as multiple-choice, and time limits) and the statistical properties of the test, especially reliability and validity. This would be a courtesy to the reader, who could also obtain this information by referring to a copy of the test and its manual.

---

[6] McMahon, West, Lewis, Armstrong, & Conway (2004, pp. 68–69).

➤ Guideline 7.8   If an unpublished instrument was used, consider reproducing sample questions or the entire instrument in the report.

For specialized research purposes, researchers often have to construct their own instruments (e.g., tests, scales, and checklists). If such an instrument is very short, a copy may be included in the research report. Longer instruments should be included in appendices in term projects, theses, and dissertations, but usually are not included in research reports published in journal articles. Authors of journal articles should be prepared to supply copies of longer, unpublished instruments to readers who request them. When it will not violate test security, providing sample items from the instrument is a good way to increase the operationalization of the variable measured with longer instruments. Example 7.8.1 is from a journal article in which the researchers describe new scales that they developed for their research. They give sample items to help operationalize their meanings of "family support" and "general peer support."

Example 7.8.1

Family support. This 8-item scale assessed participants' perceived family support during college.... Sample items included "If I needed my family for support and understanding, they would be there for me" and "My family really doesn't understand Geneseo's college environment and the type of stress that I am under" (reverse coded).

General peer support. This 8-item scale assessed participants' perceptions of peer support.... Sample items included "The friendships I have developed at Geneseo are personally satisfying" and "Few of the Geneseo students that I know would be willing to listen to me and help me if I had a personal problem (reverse coded).[7]

➤ Guideline 7.9   Operational definitions should be sufficiently specific so that another researcher can replicate the study.

A replication is an attempt to reproduce the results of a previous study by using the same research methods. Replicability is the major

---

[7] Schneider & Ward (2003, p. 543).

criterion for judging the reliability and validity of the results of empirical research.

Even definitions that appear to be highly operational at first glance may be inadequate when one attempts to replicate a study. The definition in Example 7.9.1 illustrates this point. When a researcher prepares to replicate a study involving "visual acuity," questions about the physical process arise: How large were the letters? What type of screen was used? What type of film was used to produce the letters? and so on. Answers to these questions could easily affect individuals' ability to recognize letters of the alphabet flashed on a screen.

Example 7.9.1

Visual acuity was defined as the ability to name the letters of the alphabet when flashed on a screen in a random order for a period of two seconds for each letter.

This guideline is often not followed to the letter. In practice, a writer must consider how operational a definition needs to be to permit a reasonably close replication. For making fine discriminations among very similar shapes, answers to the questions posed above about Example 7.9.1 may be crucial to a successful replication.

➢ Guideline 7.10   Even a highly operational definition may not be a useful definition.

An operational definition that is too narrow or is too far afield from how others define a variable may be inadequate. Example 7.10.1 illustrates this point. It is fairly operational, but the definition of "self-concept" is much more narrow than that used by most psychologists and teachers.

Example 7.10.1

Self-concept was defined as the number of times each child smiled during the first 15 minutes of homeroom for five consecutive days. A smile was defined as a noticeable upward turn where the lips meet—based on agreement by three independent observers. Each observer was a graduate student in clinical psychology. Counts of smiles were made from videotapes, which permitted the observers to reexamine facial expressions that were questionable.

Concluding Comments

Writing satisfactory operational definitions is sometimes more difficult than it might appear at first. When writing them, assume that you are telling someone exactly how to conduct your study. Then have your definitions reviewed by colleagues and ask them if they could perform the same study in the same way without requesting additional information.

Exercise for Chapter 7

PART A: For each of the following definitions, describe what additional types of information, if any, are needed to make it more operational.

1. Language skill was defined as scores on a scale from one to ten on an essay test that required students to write three essays in a 50-minute class period.

2. Depression was defined as the raw score on the Second Edition of Araron's Depression Inventory for Adults (Araron, 2004).

3. Computer phobia was defined as clear signs of anxiety when being seated in front of a computer.

4. Hispanic students were defined as those students whose surnames appeared on a master list of Hispanic/Latino/a surnames developed by the author in consultation with a linguist. This list may be obtained by writing to the author at P.O. Box xxx, Any City, State, Zip Code.

5. Potential high school dropouts were defined as those who have a poor attitude toward school.

6. Discrimination was defined as acts against individuals that limit their opportunities solely because of preconceived biases against the groups to which the individuals belong.

PART B: For each of the following variables, write a highly operational definition. Because you may not have studied some of these variables, do not concern yourself with whether your definitions are highly useful. (See Guideline 7.10.) Instead, make them sufficiently operational so that they would make a study of them replicable. (See Guideline 7.9.)

7. Political involvement

8. Math anxiety

9. Ability to form friendships

10. Desire to achieve in school

PART C: Name a variable you might want to study. Write a conceptual definition and a highly operational definition of it. (For this activity, do not cite a published test or scale in order to define the variable you have selected.) Have the first draft of your definitions reviewed by colleagues, and then revise them. Bring both drafts of the two definitions to class for discussion.

PART D: Examine three research articles in journals and/or theses and dissertations. Note how the variables are defined. Copy the definition you think is most operational, and bring it to class for discussion.

Chapter 8

Writing Assumptions, Limitations, and Delimitations

An *assumption* is something that is believed to be true even though the direct evidence of its truth is either absent or very limited.

A *limitation* is a weakness or handicap that potentially limits the validity of the results. A *delimitation* is a boundary to which a study was deliberately confined. To understand the difference, consider a researcher who wants to study artistic creativity in general, but uses only a measure of creative drawing. This would be a limitation because it is a weakness in the execution of the study. On the other hand, if the researcher only wants to study creative drawing and deliberately chooses a measure of this type of creativity, his or her findings would be delimited to this type of creativity, which is not a flaw in light of the researcher's purpose.

Authors of research reports published in journal articles often integrate statements of assumptions, limitations, and delimitations in various sections of their articles, including the introduction, method section, and very frequently in the discussion section at the end of the report. These authors usually are very selective in deciding which ones to state, naming only the major ones. Students who are writing term projects, theses, and dissertations are often expected to discuss these issues in some detail in order to show that they understand these concepts. In theses and dissertations, the assumptions, limitations, and delimitations are sometimes described in separate subsections of one of the chapters—often, the first chapter or the last chapter.

➤ Guideline 8.1 When stating an assumption, consider providing the reason(s) why it was necessary to make the assumption.

In Example 8.1.1, this guideline has not been followed because while it states what was assumed, it does not state why the assumption was necessary. Because no measure of human behavior is perfectly valid, Example 8.1.1 adds little to the research report. In the first sentence of the improved version, the authors describe the circumstances that led to the use of a scale that may have limited validity.

Example 8.1.1

It was assumed that the cheerfulness scale was valid.

Improved Version of Example 8.1.1

Because we did not have the resources to make direct observations and ratings of cheerfulness over time in a variety of settings, we constructed a self-report measure of cheerfulness. It was necessary to assume that the participants were honest in reporting their typical levels of cheerfulness in their self-reports. To encourage honest responses, the cheerfulness scale was administered anonymously, and the participants were encouraged to be open and honest by the research assistant who administered it.

➢ Guideline 8.2   If there is a reason for believing that an assumption is true, state the reason.

The last sentence in the Improved Version of Example 8.1.1 above suggests a basis for believing that the assumption is true. Likewise, the last sentence in Example 8.2.1 provides the basis for such a belief.

Example 8.2.1

Because the investigator could not be present in all the classrooms while the experimental method was being used, it was necessary to assume that the teachers consistently and conscientiously used the experimental method of instruction. This assumption seems tenable because the teachers were given intensive training in the method, as described in the method section of this report, and they reported enthusiasm for the method, as described in the results section.

➢ Guideline 8.3   If an assumption is highly questionable, consider casting it as a limitation.

Example 8.3.1 refers to a common flaw in research: use of a small sample. Unless a researcher has some empirical basis for believing that those in the small sample are representative of the larger population, it would be better to describe this problem as a limitation, as is done in the improved version. Note that researchers should not use assumptions to "wish away" fundamental flaws.

Example 8.3.1

It is assumed that the results we obtained with our small sample are generalizable to the larger population.

Improved Version of Example 8.3.1

Limitations and caveats need to be noted. First, our sample size was small, which may limit the generalizability of the findings.[1]

➢ Guideline 8.4   Consider speculating on the possible effects of a limitation on the results of a study.

Example 8.4.1 illustrates this guideline; the authors speculate that their results may underestimate drug use because the data was collected via face-to-face interviews. The tendency of people to underreport illegal activities is a limitation of the interview method, which can be overcome, in part, by using confidential, anonymous questionnaires.[2]

Example 8.4.1

Our findings have several limitations.... As with other interviewer-administered surveys, it is possible that personal behaviors and illegal activities such as drug use may have been underreported. Hence, our survey would have underestimated the prevalence of drug use.[3]

➢ Guideline 8.5   Discuss limitations and delimitations separately.

Because they are separate issues, discuss the *limitations* (methodological weaknesses or flaws) in separate paragraphs or sections from *delimitations* (boundaries to which the study was deliberately limited). Example 8.5.1 points out a delimitation, while Example 8.5.2 describes some limitations of the same study.

---

[1] Shadel, Niaura, & Abrams (2002, p. 175).
[2] Of course, interviews have some advantages over questionnaires, such as providing more flexibility and allowing researchers to probe for additional information.
[3] Thiede et al. (2003, p. 1920).

Example 8.5.1

Background notes on a delimitation of a study:

For a study of the effects of a domestic violence treatment program, researchers *delimited* their study to participants who had been arrested for misdemeanor domestic violence offenses. This was *not a limitation* (i.e., flaw) because the researchers were interested only in the effects of the treatment on participants who were mandated by the courts to attend the treatment program.

Example 8.5.2

Excerpt on the limitations of the study described in Example 8.5.1:

…study limitations involve the sole reliance on police records [as an outcome measure]. Actual rates of recidivism are likely to be underreported in this study. We used police records of incident reports, arrests, and convictions for DV-related [domestic-violence related] offenses. However, a relatively small proportion of domestic violence incidents results in official charges…. We did not contact the victims to assess whether the batterers committed any [additional] violent offenses that were not reported to the police…. Without partner reports, we do not know how many men continued to be involved in relationships and thus even had an opportunity to reoffend over the two years post-arrest. Ideally, we would include partners' reports of batterers' violence as a measure of recidivism, in addition to using police records. Also, in this study, rates of threats and emotional abuse are unknown. It is possible….[4]

➢ Guideline 8.6   If a study is seriously flawed by important limitations, consider labeling it as a pilot study.

A pilot study is an exploratory study that is used to try out and refine instruments, see if participants will be cooperative, check for preliminary support for a hypothesis, and so on. When this guideline is followed, it is sometimes done in the title, with a subtitle such as "A Pilot Study." Labeling a study as a pilot study can also be done in the introduction as well as in the discussion at the end of the research report.

---

[4] Babcock & Steiner (1999, p. 53).

Exercise for Chapter 8

PART A

1. Suppose you mailed a questionnaire to each member of a population but only 28% completed and returned questionnaires to you. Suppose you have no information on how the nonrespondents differ from the respondents. Would you be willing to assume that your sample is sound, *or* would you state that the nonresponse rate is a limitation? Why?

2. Suppose you administered both the experimental and control treatments to a sample of mice. You took extreme care to be sure that all mice were treated in the same way (e.g., diet, temperature, cage size, etc.) except for the administration of different treatments to the two groups. Nevertheless, you realize that there is always the potential for human error no matter how careful a researcher tries to be, and you might have unintentionally treated the experimental mice differently from the control mice. Would you state the fact that errors are always possible as an assumption, as a limitation, as a delimitation, *or* simply not refer to it in your research report? Why?

3. Suppose you used a standardized test that had been validated for the type of population you were studying. Furthermore, suppose the test had high validity but, as with all tests, was somewhat less than perfectly valid. Would you describe this circumstance as a limitation, *or* would you be willing to assume that the test is reasonably valid? Why?

PART B

4. Consider a research project that you might plan to undertake. If you know of an assumption you would probably need to make, write a statement describing it.

5. Consider a research project you might plan to undertake. If you know of a limitation (i.e., methodological flaw) that you would probably have if you conducted the study, write a statement describing it. For

the same study, describe a delimitation to which your study probably would be confined.

PART C

6. Examine three research reports published in journals and/or theses or dissertations that contain explicit statements of assumptions and/or limitations. Copy the relevant portions of them, and bring them to class for discussion.

7. How many of the individual assumptions/limitations that you examined for Question 6 involved generalizing from a sample to a population? How many involved the measuring tools or tests? How many involved the administration of experimental treatments? How many involved other issues? Name them.

Chapter 9

Writing Method Sections

The section on methods contains a description of the physical steps taken to gather data. Typically, the section begins with a description of the individuals (such as schoolchildren) or objects (such as textbooks) studied. Then the instrumentation (i.e., measuring tools) and any additional procedures (such as the administration of experimental treatments) should be described.

In reports on completed research, use the past tense to describe methods; in proposals, use the future tense.

➢ Guideline 9.1 Decide whether to use the term *subjects* or *participants* to refer to the individuals studied.

Subjects is the traditional term used to refer to individuals studied in empirical research. Increasingly, researchers are using the term *participants* to refer to these individuals. The latter term conveys the idea that these individuals freely chose to participate in a research study.[1]

When individuals freely consent to participate in a study, it seems logical to call them *participants*. Of course, informed consent is not always obtained. For instance, if you were conducting an observational study of the behavior of adolescents in a large shopping mall, you might not need consent to observe these public behaviors (although it would still be highly desirable to maintain confidentiality in your data-handling procedures). In such a study, the term *subjects* seems more appropriate because the individuals are not knowingly participating and, of course, have not consented to participate. Consent and confidentiality are discussed under the next guideline.

---

[1] Other terms that are sometimes used are *respondents* (e.g., to refer to those who respond to a mailed questionnaire) and *examinees* (e.g., to refer to those who are participating in test development research).

➢ Guideline 9.2 Describe the informed consent procedures, if any, as well as steps taken to maintain confidentiality.

Institutions such as colleges and universities as well as funding sources such as government agencies usually require researchers to obtain informed consent from the individuals who will be participating in research studies. A consent form that describes the purpose of the study, the possible benefits and harm that might result from participation, and the identification of those who are conducting the research should be prepared. Individuals are asked to sign the form acknowledging that they freely agree to participate and understand that they are free to withdraw from the study at any time without penalty.[2]

Example 9.2.1 illustrates how to briefly describe the use of informed consent in a research report. Note that the authors indicate that all those contacted signed the form. If the rate is less than 100%, the percentage or the number that signed (and, therefore, participated in the research) should be reported.

Example 9.2.1

Participants were 108 undergraduates enrolled in an introductory sociology course. Each was given an informed consent form, which had been approved by the university's institutional research review board. The form indicated that the study concerned attitudes toward road rage, that the students were not required to participate, and, if they did participate, they could withdraw from the study at any time without penalty. All students signed the form and participated fully.

Measures taken to protect the rights of participants to confidentiality are described in Example 9.2.2. Also notice that permission from the parents of minors was obtained.

Example 9.2.2

A consent form for parents to give their permission for their children to participate in the study was developed using the school district's guidelines for such forms. It was approved by the district's research and evaluation committee. Copies of the forms were mailed to the parents' homes. Permission was received by return mail for 49 out of the 50 children initially identified for participation in the study.

---

[2] Obtain precise requirements for preparing an informed consent form from your institution or funding agency.

In order to maintain confidentiality, the questionnaires were administered in the school cafeteria by a research assistant rather than the teachers. Although the teachers were present, they were instructed not to walk around the cafeteria to observe students' responses because of the sensitive nature of some of the questions. In addition, after completing the questionnaires, students folded them in half and put them into a ballot box as they filed out of the cafeteria. At no time were the teachers allowed to examine the questionnaires. As soon as the data were recorded on data collection forms and double-checked, the questionnaires were shredded. They were destroyed because some of the extended responses on the questionnaires contained information that could be used to identify individual respondents.

➢ Guideline 9.3   The participants should be described in enough detail for the reader to visualize them.

Example 9.3.1 helps readers visualize the participants' ethnicity, age, and socioeconomic status. Note that the symbol *n* stands for *number of cases* and *M* is the symbol for the *mean* (the most popular average).

Example 9.3.1

Participants were 418 sixth and seventh graders ($M = 12.4$ years) who attended an ethnically diverse middle school with a sixth-grade through eighth-grade configuration. Ethnicity of participants was determined by self-report. On the research questionnaire, students identified themselves as belonging to one of six groups that captured the range of ethnicities in the school. Twelve respondents did not answer the ethnicity question, resulting in a final sample of 406 students for this study. The ethnic breakdown of the study sample was as follows: 29.1% Latino ($n = 118$; 59 girls, 59 boys), 28.6% African American....

At the principal's request, no data on individual student socioeconomic status (SES) were gathered. In terms of school-level indicators, 68% of the students were eligible for free or reduced-price lunch programs, and the school qualified for Title I compensatory education funds. Thus, by available indicators, the school population primarily was low SES.[3]

Because the number of characteristics that might be used to describe participants is almost limitless, researchers must be highly selective in deciding on which ones to report. As a general rule, describe those that are most relevant to the issues being studied. For example, in a study on physicians' attitudes toward assisted suicide, "religious background" would be a relevant demographic variable. For a study on algebra achievement, it would not be relevant.

---

[3] Graham & Juvonen (2002, pp. 178–179).

Tables such as the one in Example 9.3.2 make it easy for readers to scan the information that describes the participants. Note the use of the term *demographic characteristics* in the title of the table. These are background characteristics that help readers visualize the participants.

Example 9.3.2

Table 1
Demographic Characteristics of the Participants

Characteristic	Number	Percent
Gender		
Girl	81	72
Boy	31	28
Current grade level		
Third	16	14
Fourth	37	33
Fifth	55	49
Sixth	4	4
Qualify for subsidized school lunch program?		
Yes	99	88
No	13	12
Family status		
Living with both parents	72	64
Living with one parent	35	31
Living with neither parent	5	4

➢ Guideline 9.4   When a sample is very small, consider providing a description of individual participants.

After summarizing in general terms the ages and psychiatric histories of ten participants in their study, the authors of Example 9.4.1 presented a table providing information on each individual. A portion of the table is shown in Example 9.4.1.

Example 9.4.1

Table 1
*Select Demographic Characteristics and Psychiatric Diagnoses
of the Participants*

Client	Age	Sex	Psychiatric diagnosis
1	25	M	Conduct disorder
			Attention deficit disorder
			Learning disability

Continued

Table 1 *continued*

Client	Age	Sex	Psychiatric diagnosis
2	19	M	Dysthymic disorder
			Major depression
3	22	F	Major depression
Etc.			

➢ Guideline 9.5   A population should be named, and if only a sample was studied, the method of sampling should be described.

Example 9.5.1 illustrates this guideline.

Example 9.5.1

From the population of all registered voters in Dallas, Texas, 250 were selected at random.

When a researcher fails to name a population, it is usually safe to assume that he or she used a sample of convenience—very often students at the college or university where the researcher is employed. Example 9.5.2, where no population is named, illustrates the common violation of this guideline.

Example 9.5.2

The sample consisted of 42 women and 34 men enrolled as students at a large public university in the southwestern United States. All participants were volunteers who had responded to a flyer seeking participants to take part in a study of sibling rivalry. The flyer indicated that the study would take about 45 minutes and that an honorarium of $10 would be paid to each participant.

➢ Guideline 9.6   Explicitly acknowledge weaknesses in sampling.

When the method of sampling is clearly deficient, such as the one in Example 9.5.2 above, it is a good idea for the author to acknowledge this fact with a sentence such as "Because a sample of convenience was used, generalizations to populations should be made with extreme caution," or "The use of volunteers as participants in this study greatly restricts the generalizability of the results." Inclusion of statements such as these is especially important in student projects, theses, and dissertations. In their absence, instructors may not know whether students are aware of this important limitation.[4]

➢ Guideline 9.7   Provide detailed information on nonparticipants when possible.

Information on individuals who refuse to participate in a study is often known and, usually, can be ethically reported on by using group averages or percentages with no identifying information on the individuals themselves. For instance, in a study in a school setting, the cumulative records of nonparticipating students might be accessed for information that would indicate differences between participants and nonparticipants.

The researcher who wrote Example 9.7.1 sent letters soliciting participation in her study to all families referred to a program for child abuse prevention in a 12-month period, but only 26% of them participated in the study. The information in the last sentence of the example helps reassure readers that nonparticipants are not substantially different from participants (i.e., helps reassure them that the nonparticipants are not an idiosyncratic subgroup of the population).

Example 9.7.1

Initial recruitment letters were sent, on a rolling basis, to all participants who had been referred to the program within a 12-month period. The letters were sent within 2 months of the referral. A second recruitment letter and a follow-up phone call followed, if needed. In 12 months, 76 referred clients were solicited for research participation; 23 responded that they were interested, with 20 ultimately participating. An analysis of this subgroup yielded no significant differences from the 56 participants who chose not to participate in terms of race, age, number of children, zip code, or socioeconomic status.[5]

➢ Guideline 9.8   If there was attrition, state the number who dropped out, the reasons for dropping out, if known, and information on the dropouts, if available.

The previous guideline refers to individuals who were asked to

---

[4] While statements regarding generalizing from a sample are often made in the Method section, many researchers also make them in the Discussion section at the end of the research report.
[5] Altman (2003, p. 472).

participate but refused. This guideline refers to the attrition of individuals who began to participate in the study but then dropped out. Attrition can make the interpretation of the results of a study difficult whenever there is the possibility that those who dropped out are different from those who remained. For instance, in a study of an experimental drug, those who dropped out of the experimental group might have been the ones who experienced serious side effects, leading the researchers to underestimate the side effects of the drug. One partial solution to this problem is to ask dropouts for the reasons why they dropped out. Of course, often not all dropouts can be located for questioning and not all are cooperative in providing such information.

Because attrition can be an important problem, the demographics and other information about dropouts should be provided, if possible. Example 9.8.1 illustrates this guideline.

Example 9.8.1

Two boys (ages 10 and 11) and three girls (all age 10) dropped out of the study because their families had moved out of the school district. All five were Latino/a and spoke English as a second language. Their percentile ranks on the *Metropolitan Reading Test* (English Version) ranged from 45 to 65, which is similar to the percentile ranks of the participants who did not drop out.

➤ Guideline 9.9 Unpublished instruments should be described in detail.

Instruments are measuring tools (such as achievement tests, attitude scales, questionnaires, checklists, and interview schedules). The instrument used to measure a construct defines it. For instance, if a researcher is studying attitudes toward capitalism, the items on the attitude scale constitute his or her definition of this type of attitude. If another researcher uses a different set of questions to measure attitudes toward capitalism, he or she will have a different definition of this construct than the first researcher. Obviously, it is important to provide readers with detailed information on the instruments, including the questions or sample questions, when possible.

Frequently, researchers have to build their own instruments because none are available for their particular research purposes. When this is done, the section on methods should provide a detailed description of the instrument. Consider Example 9.9.1, which has insufficient detail, and its improved version. Notice that the researcher has included the questionnaire in an appendix, which is desirable when space permits.

Example 9.9.1

Attitude toward school was measured with a nine-item questionnaire developed for use in this study.

Improved Version of Example 9.9.1

Attitude toward school was measured with a questionnaire developed for use in this study. It contains nine statements. The first three measure attitudes toward academic subjects; the next three measure attitudes toward teachers, counselors, and administrators; the last three measure attitudes toward the social environment in the school. Participants were asked to rate each statement on a five-point scale from 1 (strongly disagree) to 5 (strongly agree). The complete questionnaire is shown in Appendix A of this journal article.

➢ Guideline 9.10   If a published instrument was used, briefly describe the traits it was designed to measure, its format, and the possible range of score values.

There is less obligation for a researcher to describe in detail a published instrument than an unpublished instrument because published instruments are usually available for inspection by other researchers. Nevertheless, as a courtesy to their readers, researchers should provide some general information about published instruments, such as those elements named in this guideline.

➢ Guideline 9.11   For both unpublished and published instruments, information on reliability and validity, when available, should be reported.

The two most important characteristics of an instrument are its reliability (consistency of results) and validity (the extent to which the instrument measures what it is designed to measure). For published instruments that are well known and in widespread use, it is sometimes sufficient to refer only briefly to the availability of reliability and validity information in other published sources such as journal articles and test manuals.

In Example 9.11.1, the researchers name the traits the survey scale is designed to measure. Then they provide specific statistics on internal consistency and reliability (i.e., a test–retest reliability coefficient of .78). They conclude by giving a reference where information on its validity can be found.

Example 9.11.1

The MOS Social Support Survey (Sherbourne & Stewart, 1991) measures four dimensions of social support.... The MOS Social Support Survey offers excellent reliability, with high internal consistency for the overall scale ($\alpha = .97$) and the subscales...plus a high 1-year test–retest reliability at .78. Criterion validity has been documented (McDowell & Newell, 1996).[6]

For less well known published as well as unpublished instruments, more detail on these issues is desirable, especially if other sources of information about them are limited or nonexistent.

Students who are writing theses and dissertations may be expected to describe the reliability and validity of the instruments they use in considerable detail. They may be expected, for example, to summarize how the reliability and validity studies were conducted and to interpret the results of these studies in light of any methodological flaws in the studies.

➢ Guideline 9.12   Experimental procedures, equipment, and other mechanical matters should be described in sufficient detail so that the study can be replicated.

Some subjectivity enters into deciding how much detail to provide. In most cases, authors of journal articles do not provide every detail. Instead, they try to provide enough information to permit a reasonably close replication. Example 9.12.1 shows a description that might permit a rough replication, especially because the test used as part of the stimulus materials is published and available to other researchers.

Example 9.12.1

All groups took the Connors Continuous Performance Test II (Connors & MHS Staff, 2000). The test requires the individual to respond to simple visual cues (pressing a button every time they see a letter except for the letter X).
    Subjects in [one group] were told: "You are going to take a test to see how distracting other passengers in the car are. You will take a test where you have to

---

[6] Hughes, Nosek, Howland, Groff, & Mullen (2003, pp. 183–184).

press the spacebar when you see every letter except X while I sit here and ask you simple questions." The questions asked during the test were standard questions given in the same order for each subject, asking for demographic information and personal information such as someone's favorite movie.[7]

Generally, more detail on experimental procedures, equipment, and other mechanical matters are expected in term projects, theses, and dissertations than in journal articles because students are expected to show that they can write precise, detailed descriptions.

Exercise for Chapter 9

PART A

1. According to this chapter, what idea is conveyed by the term "participants"?

2. Consider Examples 9.2.1 and 9.2.2. In your opinion, would it have been as effective simply to say that "participants signed an institutionally approved consent form and confidentiality was maintained" without the other details? Explain.

3. Name at least two demographic variables not mentioned in this chapter that researchers could measure and describe in their research reports.

4. According to this chapter, should demographics always be reported in terms of group statistics such as percentages and averages?

5. Consider Example 9.5.2. In your opinion, how important is this description of the method of recruitment of the participants? Explain.

6. In research, what does "attrition" refer to?

7. What two types of information should be reported for both unpublished and published instruments? (Hint: The two most important characteristics of an instrument.)

---

[7] Golden, Golden, & Schneider (2003, pp. 386–387).

PART B

8. Locate a description of participants in a research report in a journal article, thesis, or dissertation that you think lacks sufficient detail. Copy it, and briefly describe other types of information that might have been included to give a better picture of the participants. Bring your work to class for discussion.

9. Locate a description of the instrumentation in a research report in a journal article, thesis, or dissertation that describes its reliability and validity. Bring it to class for discussion.

10. Locate a description of the procedures, equipment, and other mechanical matters in a research report in a journal article, thesis, or dissertation. Bring it to class for discussion. Be prepared to discuss whether the description is sufficiently detailed.

Notes:

Chapter 10

Writing Analysis and Results Sections

The analysis and results section usually follows the section on methods. In a proposal, the proposed method of analysis should be described; the anticipated results may also be discussed.

➤ Guideline 10.1   Organize the analysis and results section around the research hypotheses, purposes, or questions stated in the introduction.

This is an overarching guideline that helps your readers understand the organization of your results. Example 10.1.1 shows the three research questions posed in the introduction to a research report on economically disadvantaged preschoolers. It also shows a portion of the results. Notice how the results are organized around the three research questions.

Example 10.1.1

Research questions posed in the introduction:

Specifically, three questions guided this research: (a) Is parental involvement associated with program effectiveness in terms of students' achievement? (b) Is parental involvement associated with attendance rates? and (c) Is parental involvement associated with their children's desire to continue to take part in the program?

Portions of the results section, which illustrate the organization around the three research questions:

The first research question concerned the possible association between parental involvement and students' achievement. Table 1 shows the means and standard deviations on three achievement tests for two groups of students: students whose parents were highly involved and students whose parents were less involved. A statistically significant difference was found between....

To examine the second research question, parents' scores on the involvement scale were correlated with their children's attendance in program sessions. Specifically, the involvement scores were correlated with number of days attended. This analysis indicated that parents' involvement was significantly correlated with....

The third research question concerned the association between parental involvement and children's desire to continue to take part in the program. The analysis of the data on this question revealed....

➤ Guideline 10.2   Standard statistical procedures need only be named; it is usually not necessary to show formulas or calculations.

Likewise, it is usually unnecessary to name the particular computer program used to perform the analysis.

➤ Guideline 10.3   The scores of individual participants usually are not shown; instead, statistics based on the scores should be reported.

Suppose you had tested a random sample of 50 students in an elementary school with a standardized achievement test battery. Normally, you would *not* list the scores of individual children. Instead, you would provide summary statistics such as the mean and standard deviation. Note, however, that some instructors may require students who are writing term projects, theses, and dissertations to include participants' scores in an appendix so that the instructor can check the analysis.

➤ Guideline 10.4   Present descriptive statistics first.

For each set of continuous scores, provide information on central tendency and variability (usually means and standard deviations) before presenting correlation coefficients, if any, and the results of inferential statistical tests such as the *t* test. For example, correlation coefficients may provide direct information on a research hypothesis; even if this is the case, report measures of central tendency and variability first. These measures will show your reader what the average participant was like and how variable the group was.

For categorical (nominal) data, present frequencies and percentages before presenting the results of inferential statistical tests such as the chi square test.

➤ Guideline 10.5 Organize large numbers of statistics in tables, and give each table a number and descriptive title (i.e., caption).

Tables are especially effective for helping readers compare groups. The table in Example 10.5.1 makes it easy to compare the ages of women and men.

Example 10.5.1

Table 1
Percentages of Women and Men in Various Age Groups

Age	Women ($n = 830$)	Men ($n = 723$)
18 years and under	4.8% ($n = 40$)	8.7% ($n = 63$)
19–24 years	9.9% ($n = 82$)	13.3% ($n = 96$)
25–34 years	18.2% ($n = 151$)	25.4% ($n = 184$)
35–44 years	22.8% ($n = 189$)	19.4% ($n = 140$)
45–54 years	20.0% ($n = 166$)	15.4% ($n = 111$)
55–64 years	13.7% ($n = 114$)	13.8% ($n = 100$)
65–74 years	5.3% ($n = 44$)	2.6% ($n = 19$)
75 years and over	5.3% ($n = 44$)	1.4% ($n = 10$)
Total	100.0%	100.0%

The titles of tables (also known as *captions*) should name the statistics presented in the table and the variables that were studied. Example 10.5.2 shows four titles that do this.

Example 10.5.2

Table 1 *Number and Percentage of Participants by Gender and Welfare Status*

Table 2 *Means and Standard Deviations on Reading and Mathematics*

Table 3 *Intercorrelation Matrix for Voting-Behavior Variables*

Table 4 *Analysis of Variance for Mathematics Scores*

When separate tables are presented for two or more groups, the title of each table should also name the group. Example 10.5.3 shows the titles of tables for two different groups.

Example 10.5.3

Table 1 *Intercorrelation Matrix of Middle-Level Managers' Personality Scores*

Table 2 *Intercorrelation Matrix of Chief Executive Officers' Personality Scores*

➢ Guideline 10.6   When describing the statistics presented in a table, point out only the highlights.

Briefly describe the important points in each table you present. Because the values of the statistics are presented in a table, it is not necessary to repeat each value in your discussion of the results. This is illustrated in Example 10.6.1, which shows a statistical table, and Example 10.6.2, which shows the discussion of it. Note that in the discussion only certain specific statistics are mentioned in order to assist the reader in getting an overview of the tabled results.

Example 10.6.1

Table 1
Percentage of Substance Use in Past Month of Urban and Suburban Samples

	Drug A		Drug B		Drug C	
Grade	Urban	Suburban	Urban	Suburban	Urban	Suburban
11	33.6	23.2	13.1	14.0	5.2	4.3
12	34.2	24.1	13.9	13.8	4.7	4.8

Example 10.6.2

Table 1 shows the percentage of urban and suburban 11th and 12th graders who reported using three illicit drugs during the previous month. Overall, Drug A had the highest percentages reporting its use, with percentages for subgroups ranging from 23.2% to 34.2%. Use of Drug B was reported by much smaller percentages of students (from 13.1% to 14.0% for subgroups). Use of Drug C was reported by relatively small percentages of students, with the highest percentage being 5.2% for urban 11th graders. Consistent with the hypothesis, the most striking difference between urban and suburban students was in the reported usage of Drug A, with more than 10% more urban students than suburban students reporting its use.

➢ Guideline 10.7   Statistical figures (i.e., drawings such as bar graphs) should be professionally drawn and used sparingly in journal articles.

Figures may be used to organize and describe data. They usually take up more space, however, than would a corresponding statistical table. Because space in journals is limited, figures should be used sparingly. In term projects, theses, and dissertations, where space is not an issue, they may be used more frequently.

Because figures attract the eye better than tables, their best use is to present important data, especially striking data that might otherwise be overlooked in a table of statistical values. Example 10.7.1 shows such a figure, which illustrates a striking difference between the experimental groups and the control group on a scale from zero (no improvement) to 50 (outstanding improvement).

Like statistical tables, statistical figures should be numbered and given captions (titles) that name the variables and the statistics presented, which is done in the following example. Typically, figure numbers and titles are placed *below* the figures. For tables, they are placed *above*.

Example 10.7.1

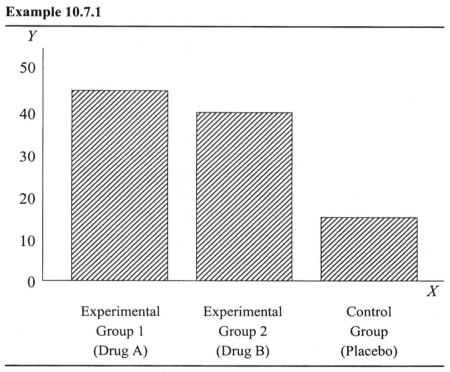

Figure 1. Mean improvement scores for three groups.

➢ Guideline 10.8 Statistical symbols should be underlined or italicized.

In Example 10.8.1, the statistical symbols (i.e., *t*, *df*, and *p*) are italicized. Without italics, "p" is just the letter "p." With italics, "*p*" stands for "probability." If you do not have the ability to italicize, underline the symbols; typesetters recognize underlining as a direction to italicize.

Example 10.8.1

The mean of the experimental group was significantly higher than the mean of the control group ($t = 2.310$, $df = 10$, $p < .05$, two tailed).

➢ Guideline 10.9   Use the proper case for each statistical symbol.

As statistical symbols, upper- and lowercase letters often stand for entirely different statistics. For example, a lowercase "f" stands for "frequency," while an uppercase "F" is an inferential statistic used in significance testing. Also, a lowercase "t" is the symbol for a statistic frequently used to test the difference between two means, while an uppercase "T" is a special type of standardized test score.

For some statistics, the upper- and lowercases stand for the same statistic but communicate important information about sampling, in which the lowercase indicates that the value is an estimate based on a sample while the uppercase indicates that the value is based on a population. For instance, researchers use "m" to stand for an estimated mean (an average) based on a sample but use "M" to stand for the mean when it is based on the population. The same is true for the symbols for the standard deviation ("s" and "S") and for number of cases ("n" for the number in a sample and "N" for the number in a population).[1]

➢ Guideline 10.10   Spell out numbers that are less than ten. Spell out numbers that start sentences.

The main exceptions to this guideline are when referring to elements in a numbered list such as "Chapter 1" and "Chapter 2" and when presenting precise numerical results (e.g., "The median equals 8").

---

[1] Symbols used for the mean and standard deviation may vary among researchers. Because statistics textbooks often use X-bar (an X with a bar over it) as the symbol for the mean, a small percentage of researchers use it instead of m or M in their research reports. In addition, some researchers prefer to use sd and SD instead of s or S as the symbol for the standard deviation.

➢ Guideline 10.11 Qualitative results should be organized and the organization made clear to the reader.

In qualitative studies, statistics are usually not reported. Instead, researchers report on major trends and themes that emerged from subjective and objective analyses of data such as transcribed interviews. The presentation of such results should be organized; consider using subheadings to guide the reader through the results. This is illustrated in Example 10.11.1, which is the first paragraph in the results section of a report on a qualitative study. Note that it provides readers with a description of the organization of the results. The remaining portion of the results (not shown in the example) is divided into three parts with subheadings suggested in the example (e.g., Educational Aspirations of Parents and Youth).

Example 10.11.1

Key findings of the current study are divided into three sections. The first section addresses parents' educational and occupational aspirations, as well as those of their youth. The second section discusses parental knowledge of youth aspirations. The final section delineates the barriers to attainment of aspirations from parent and youth perspectives, and their input on what resources they needed to attain their aspirations.[2]

See Chapter 13 for additional guidelines on reporting the results of qualitative research.

Exercise for Chapter 10

PART A

1. An "overarching guideline" for the organization of the analysis and results section is to organize them around what?

2. Is it usually necessary to show formulas and calculations in the analysis and results section of a research report?

---

[2] Behnke, Piercy, & Diversi (2004, pp. 21–22).

3. Should "descriptive statistics" *or* "inferential statistics" usually be presented first?

4. The titles of tables (i.e., captions) should name what two things?

5. Should all the values in statistical tables be described in the narrative of the report? Explain.

6. How does "p" differ from "*p*" in terms of their meanings?

7. How does "*n*" differ from "*N*" in terms of their meanings?

PART B

8. Examine the results sections of two research reports published in journals. Determine whether the authors followed Guideline 10.4. Be prepared to discuss your findings in class.

9. Locate a statistical table in a published article that you think has a good title (i.e., caption). Copy it, and bring it to class for discussion.

10. Locate a statistical figure in a research report published in a journal. Discuss whether presentation in the form of a table of statistical values would have been as effective as presentation of the figure.

Chapter 11

Writing Discussion Sections

This chapter presents guidelines for writing the last section of a research report in a journal article or the last chapter of a thesis or dissertation, which typically begins with one of various headings such as *Summary and Discussion, Discussion and Conclusions, Conclusions and Implications*, or simply the term *Discussion*.

➢ Guideline 11.1   Consider starting the discussion with a summary.

Authors of long research reports, theses, and dissertations often begin their discussion section with a summary of the highlights of the material that preceded it. For short reports, a summary is usually not necessary.

➢ Guideline 11.2   Early in the discussion section, refer to the research hypotheses, purposes, or questions stated in the introduction.

Briefly restate the hypotheses, purposes, or questions and indicate whether the data support the hypotheses, whether the research purposes were achieved, or what answers were obtained for the research questions. Of course, you did this in the results section also—probably in some detail with a number of statistics. In the discussion, do not repeat all the details. Instead, reiterate only the highlights.

Following this guideline helps to refocus readers' attention on the fundamental purposes of the research report and sets the stage for other aspects of the discussion.

➢ Guideline 11.3 Point out whether results of the current study are consistent with the results and theories described in the introduction.

Because the review of the literature near the beginning of a research report helps set the stage for the current study, it is important to discuss at the end how the current findings relate to those reported earlier in the literature review as well as how they relate to theories described in the introduction. This is illustrated in Example 11.3.1 in which the researchers note that their results are inconsistent with those of an earlier study, which they described in the introduction to their research report. In contrast, they note that their results are consistent with a theory (i.e., they say that their results provide some support for the theory). The theory was first discussed in the introduction to the research report.

Example 11.3.1

Our findings indicate that the image of God as being present, accepting, and offering challenge to one's growth in life is associated with greater incidence of both religious practices and religiously motivated volitional behaviors. These data, thus, appear to provide preliminary evidence that, contrary to the findings of Lee and Early (2000), God-image and religious behavior are not independent of each other when....

These data appear to provide some support for the assertions of attachment theorists, that subjects' perceptions of God as a "stronger, wise, other" who is lovingly present would be associated with greater attachment to God via religious behavior. In particular....[1]

In the introduction to their research report, the authors of Example 11.3.2 discuss the fact that most of the previous research on gender differences in perceived attractiveness and body weight involved girls and women, especially female undergraduates and adolescents. They point out, however, that there is some "indirect" evidence that overweight women are less likely to be satisfied with their weight than overweight men. The example is drawn from the discussion section of their research report in which they used adults aged 20 to 29 as participants. As you can see, the researchers have come full circle by reviewing in their discussion section an important issue raised in their introduction.

---

[1] Buchko & Witzig (2003, p. 1146).

Example 11.3.2

A significant proportion of normal-weight men felt they were underweight, and an even larger percentage of overweight men thought they were normal weight. The opposite emerged for women: A large number of normal-weight women felt they were overweight. These findings support those from research with adolescents and university students, suggesting that weight misperceptions evident in early through late adolescence are also found in adults.[2]

➢ Guideline 11.4   Consider interpreting the results and offering explanations for them in the discussion section.

Following this guideline helps readers understand the results and put them in context. Since interpretations and explanations go beyond the data actually collected, researchers should be careful not to imply that they are data-based explanations; rather, they are possible explanations that are consistent with the data. The authors of Example 11.4.1 offer an explanation of their findings.

Example 11.4.1

It is interesting to speculate on possible reasons why the fear levels expressed by the 10-year-old children were so much greater than those expressed by the 8-year-old children in this study. One possibility is that the younger children did not have the conceptual background to fully understand the presentation made in the experimental setting. Specifically, they might have....

It is especially desirable to offer possible explanations for unexpected findings. In Example 11.4.2, the researchers were surprised to find that residential instability did not predict behavior problems in a sample of children age six and older.

Example 11.4.2

To our surprise, residential instability did not predict behavior problems and, in fact, children who had moved more often in the past year were less likely to have either internalizing or externalizing behavior problems.... Although not a definitive finding, a possible explanation is that some children may habituate to residential instability and be less affected by moving to a shelter than children who have experienced greater housing stability prior to becoming homeless.[3]

---

[2] McCreary & Sadava (2001, p. 113).
[3] Buckner, Bassuk, Weinreb, & Brooks (1999, p. 253).

➢ Guideline 11.5   Mention important strengths and limitations in the discussion.

Strengths and limitations of the research methodology are sometimes first mentioned in the introduction or the section on methods. Because strengths and limitations can affect the interpretations of data described in the discussion section, it is usually appropriate to mention the most important ones in the discussion. The authors of Example 11.5.1 point out some strengths of their study. By pointing out that a study is especially strong methodologically, researchers encourage their readers to give more credence to their study, which is especially important if there are conflicting conclusions reached in weaker studies.

Example 11.5.1

The current study has several strengths. It collected information on IPV [intimate partner violence] from both partners, which enhances the probability of identification of spousal violence.... [In addition,] interviews with Hispanics were conducted in English or Spanish, which allows for inclusion of bilingual and monolingual respondents. [Third,] the longitudinal design allows for the assessment of incidence and recurrence of violence.[4]

Example 11.5.2 shows a statement regarding the limitations of a study. A frank discussion of limitations helps warn readers to be cautious in drawing conclusions from a study.

Example 11.5.2

Some limitations of the present research design...should be addressed. The samples were only Japanese university students, so the validity of the findings in different cultural settings is unknown. The present findings were based on university students' responses, not those of practicing managers and employees. In addition, students reported what they imagined they would do, not what they would actually do.[5]

Students who are writing theses and dissertations should provide detailed descriptions of the limitations of their research. Such statements will help to reassure their committee members that the students are knowledgeable of important methodological issues in their research. Students who are writing research reports as term projects should determine how detailed their professors want their discussions to be.

---

[4] Caetano, Ramisetty-Mikler, & McGrath (2004, p. 75).
[5] Matsui, Kakuyama, & Tsuzuki (2003, p. 1139).

➢ Guideline 11.6   It is usually inappropriate to introduce new data or new references in the discussion section.

The discussion section of a research report should be used to summarize and interpret what was presented earlier. The introduction of new data or references distracts from this purpose.

➢ Guideline 11.7   When possible, state specific implications in the discussion section.

The implications of a study are usually cast in the form of actions that individuals or organizations should take based on the results of the study. In Example 11.7.1, the researchers state an implication for burn teams that treat individuals with burn injuries.

Example 11.7.1

Our findings further suggest that psychological complaints are more prevalent than physical ones after burn injuries. This highlights the importance of burn teams attending to the needs of the "whole patient" rather than simply to physical domains. With the passage of time, important concerns such as unhappiness with appearance, posttraumatic stress, sleep problems, and sexual dysfunction may be increasingly salient but underaddressed patient concerns.[6]

After presenting data indicating that family factors are important in retaining soldiers as well as in supervisors' ratings of the soldiers, the authors of Example 11.7.2 (which is from the discussion section of their report) suggest a practical implication for the military. Note that they did not study their suggestion for giving soldiers adjusted schedules so that they could take care of family matters. Instead, the researchers are suggesting that this is a logical implication of their results.

Example 11.7.2

For example, leaders might allow a soldier time off for a child's dental appointment, while a post commander might designate Thursday afternoon after 1500 hours as a commander's time for family support. In addition, giving most soldiers time during normal working hours to handle family business [and] making work schedules as predictable as possible...are useful ways to improve

---

[6] Williams, Doctor, Patterson, & Gibran (2003, p. 193).

the quality of military family life.... Morale can be improved by ensuring that soldiers are aware that leaders really do care about family concerns....[7]

If you have conducted a pilot study, you probably should hedge in your statement of implications by beginning the statement with a caution such as the one shown in Example 11.7.3.

Example 11.7.3

If the results obtained in this pilot study are confirmed in more definitive studies, the following implications should be considered by....

In a proposal, you should discuss the possible implications of the study. Sometimes this is done in the introduction, and sometimes it is done in the discussion section of a proposal. Example 11.7.4 shows how this might begin.

Example 11.7.4

If the research hypothesis is supported by the data collected in the proposed study, the implications will be as follows....

➤ Guideline 11.8   Be specific when making recommendations for future research.

It is uninformative to end a research report with a vague statement such as "Further research is needed." Instead, researchers should point out what specific directions this research might take in order to advance knowledge of a topic. Examples 11.8.1 and 11.8.2 illustrate the degree of specificity often found in research reports published in journal articles.

Example 11.8.1

Future research on tutorials such as the one used in the present study is needed to investigate several factors, including the following: (a) Which components of the tutorial contribute to its effectiveness? (b) What roles do social features of the tutorials play in children's progress? For example, does language that suggests a warm and caring tutor disposition tend to positively affect children's development more than on-task, take-charge directive language? and (c) Does tutor experience play a role? For example, do children tutored by tutors who continue from year to year tend to do better than others?[8]

---

[7] Schumm, Bell, & Resnick (2001, p. 163).
[8] Fitzgerald (2001, p. 45).

Example 11.8.2

Further research should be directed at replication of the present study using a larger sample of Chinese adolescents in order to explore and understand their development more thoroughly. Moreover, a comparison of Chinese family environment and adolescent coping style with those of Western cultures would be useful in delineating universal as well as culture-specific components.

In addition, research should focus on examining various family-adolescent relationships when adolescents are in stressful circumstances....[9]

If you are writing a thesis or dissertation, you might be expected to discuss your suggestions for future research in more detail than shown in Examples 11.8.1 and 11.8.2.

Exercise for Chapter 11

PART A

1. According to this chapter, should discussion sections always begin with a summary? Explain.

2. Should writers refer to the literature cited at the beginning of their reports in their discussion sections? Why? Why not?

3. Is it acceptable for researchers to offer explanations for their results that go beyond the data actually analyzed?

4. Is it usually appropriate to introduce new references in the discussion section of a research report?

5. Is it appropriate for researchers to describe possible implications of their results, *or* should they just restrict themselves to an objective discussion of the actual data?

6. According to this chapter, is it appropriate to end a research report with only this sentence: "Further research is needed."? Explain.

---

[9] Hamid, Yue, & Leung (2003, p. 127).

PART B

7. Read three research articles published in journals and/or theses or dissertations, and examine the discussion sections of them carefully.

   a. In how many do the authors discuss the consistency of their results with previously published results?

   b. In how many do the authors mention important strengths and weaknesses of their studies?

   c. In how many do the authors introduce new data or new references?

   d. In how many do the authors explicitly state the implications of their results?

8. Compare the three discussion sections you examined for Question 7, and select the one you think is the best. Copy it, and bring it to class for discussion.

Chapter 12

Writing Abstracts

An abstract is a summary of the report that is placed below the title in a journal article. In a thesis or dissertation, it is usually placed on a separate page following the title page.

➢ Guideline 12.1   In the abstract, refer to the research hypotheses, purposes, or questions.

Researchers often begin their abstracts with very brief statements of their research hypotheses, purposes, or questions. Examples 12.1.1 and 12.1.2 show the beginnings of two abstracts that follow this guideline.

Example 12.1.1
The hypothesis that High and Low Spiritual Well-Being groups have different personality profiles was tested with 319 psychology undergraduates....[1]

Example 12.1.2
The purpose was to examine whether Japanese individuals were oriented toward collective and masculine values attributed to cultures....[2]

➢ Guideline 12.2   Highlights of the methodology should be summarized.

Information on methodology (such as how variables were measured or what treatments were given in an experiment) helps potential readers determine whether the report will be of interest to them. Example 12.2.1 shows a complete abstract. Notice that the second through fourth sentences describe research methodology.

---

[1] Ramanaiah, Rielage, & Sharpe (2001, p. 659).
[2] Hirokawa, Dohi, Vannieuwenhuyse, & Miyata (2001, p. 243).

Example 12.2.1

The authors evaluated the effect of listening to stories on children's vocabulary growth. Forty-seven children listened to 2 stories read to them in a small-group setting on 3 occasions, each 1 week apart. Target vocabulary items and items assessing generalization to nontarget words were selected, and pre- and posttest multiple-choice vocabulary measures were designed to measure vocabulary gains. In addition, a reading–retelling task was used to measure the subjects' knowledge of target and generalization words. For 1 story, children listened to the reading and were given explanations of target word meanings; for the other, children were not given explanations. The children acquired new vocabulary from listening to stories, with both frequency of exposure and teacher explanation of the target words enhancing vocabulary learning. However, the interventions were not sufficient to overcome the Matthew effect, as the higher-ability children made greater vocabulary gains than lower-ability children across all conditions.[3]

➢ Guideline 12.3   Highlights of the results should be included in the abstract.

In Example 12.2.1 above, the results are mentioned in the last two sentences. In Example 12.3.1, the abstract provides a more detailed description of the results. Notice that the authors of both examples begin with references to their purpose, followed by information on their research methods, and end with information on their results. This arrangement is recommended.

Example 12.3.1

The use of the telephone has become an increasingly popular mode for providing counseling. However, little is known about its effectiveness. This study is an initial effectiveness study on telephone counseling. Participants ($N = 186$) who had received counseling from a telephone counseling service rated the effectiveness of telephone counseling and the quality of their counseling relationship. Generally, respondents indicated that telephone counseling was helpful for both global and specific improvement and that they were satisfied with the counseling they received. Respondents also rated the counseling relationship and level of interpersonal influence similarly to face-to-face counseling studies measuring the same attributes. The telephone counseling results are given in the context of face-to-face counseling data from other studies.[4]

---

[3] Penno, Wilkinson, & Moore (2002, p. 23).
[4] Reese, Conoley, & Brossart (2002, p. 233).

➢ Guideline 12.4 If a study is based on a theory, name the theory in the abstract.

Typically, theories provide principles that help explain a wide variety of observations. For example, social learning theory applies to a large number of phenomena observed in teaching and learning studies. When the results of individual studies are consistent with predictions based on a theory, they lend support to the theory. On the other hand, when results of individual studies are inconsistent with a theory, the theory, or at least portions of it, should be reconsidered.

Because of the importance of theories in advancing knowledge, they are sometimes mentioned in the titles of research articles. More often, they are mentioned in the abstracts. Examples 12.4.1 and 12.4.2 illustrate how to follow this guideline. Note that less-encompassing "theories" are sometimes called "models."

Example 12.4.1

The authors examined the effects of both general and task-specific writing experiences on college students' writing-skill development. On the basis of theories of expertise development and a cognitive process theory of writing-skill development, the authors predicted that repeated practice would be associated with superior writing skills and that after controlling for repeated practice, writing within a specific task domain would be associated with superior writing skills. Undergraduate students participated in a field experiment in which 279 students practiced their writing skills in a professionally relevant task domain, whereas another group of 385 students practiced their writing skills in a more general domain. The results were consistent with the predictions. The authors discuss implications for teaching writing skills and for general theories of expertise development in writing.[5]

Example 12.4.2

The authors investigated whether people can feel happy and sad at the same time. J. A. Russell and J. M. Carroll's (1999) circumplex model holds that happiness and sadness are polar opposites and, thus, mutually exclusive. In contrast, the evaluative space model (J. T. Cacioppo, & G. G. Berntson, 1994) proposes that positive and negative affect are separable and that mixed feelings of happiness and sadness can co-occur. The authors both replicated and extended past research by showing that whereas most participants surveyed in typical situations felt either happy or sad, many participants surveyed immediately after watching the film *Life Is Beautiful*, moving out of their dormitories, or graduating from college felt both happy and sad. Results suggest that although affective experience may

---

[5] Johnstone, Ashbaugh, & Warfield (2002, p. 305).

typically be bipolar, the underlying processes, and occasionally the resulting experience of emotion, are better characterized as bivariate.[6]

Notice that Examples 12.4.1 and 12.4.2 are of typical length for journal articles.

➢ Guideline 12.5   An abstract should usually be short; however, there are exceptions.

Many journals limit the number of words that may be included in abstracts—some as short as 200 or less. For instance, journals published by the American Psychological Association limit abstracts to a maximum of 120 words. Example 12.5.1 shows the suggested organization for a short abstract. Some journals encourage long abstracts. Students who are writing theses and dissertations should determine their institution's requirements regarding length and number of words. When long abstracts are permitted (or required), consider incorporating information on the importance of the problem and the implications of the results in addition to the other elements mentioned in the earlier guidelines in this chapter. In a long abstract, you may want to use subheadings such as those shown in Example 12.5.2.

Example 12.5.1

Suggested elements to cover in a short abstract (no subheadings):

1. Research hypotheses, purposes, or questions. These may need to be abbreviated or summarized if they are extensive.
2. Highlights of the research methods.
3. Highlights of the results.

Example 12.5.2

Suggested elements to cover in a long abstract (subheadings shown in italics):

1. *Background*
   Describe the problem area and its importance.
2. *Research Hypotheses*
   (or *Research Purposes* or *Research Questions*)
3. *Method*
4. *Results*
5. *Implications*
6. *Suggestions for Further Research*

---

[6] Larsen, McGraw, & Cacioppo (2001, p. 684).

The amount of emphasis to put on each element in an abstract is a subjective matter. When writing it, keep in mind that your goal is to provide enough information for potential readers to make informed decisions on whether to read your entire research report or not. Elements that make your research unique generally deserve more emphasis than other elements. For instance, if you are the first to conduct a true experiment on a problem, be sure to point it out in the abstract.

Exercise for Chapter 12

PART A

1. Generally, with what should a typical abstract (not a long one) start?

2. In light of this chapter, would you expect to find highlights of the research methodology described in an abstract?

3. Should highlights of the results be included in an abstract?

4. If a study is based on a theory, should this fact be mentioned in the abstract?

5. Are there any major deficiencies in the following abstract? Explain.

    Abstract: Two hundred second-grade students were administered a battery of published cognitive tests that measured a variety of academic achievement variables. The students were drawn from 3 elementary schools in a large, urban school district. All were tested near the end of second grade. Test administrators administered the tests in 3 sessions because students might become fatigued by taking the entire battery in a single testing session. The 3 research hypotheses were confirmed. Implications for cognitive development and directions for future research are discussed.

PART B: Locate an abstract for a research report published in a journal that you believe illustrates the guidelines in this chapter. Bring a copy to class for discussion.

PART C: Locate a research report published in a journal, and read the article without reading the abstract. Write your own abstract for the article, and compare it with the abstract prepared by the author(s) of the article.

Chapter 13

A Closer Look at Writing Reports of Qualitative Research

With certain obvious exceptions such as some of the guidelines on reporting statistical results, the guidelines in the previous chapters should be considered when writing reports of qualitative research. This chapter presents guidelines that are specific to reporting qualitative research.

➤ Guideline 13.1   Consider using the term "qualitative" in the title or abstract of the report.

Because the vast majority of research in the social and behavioral sciences continues to be *quantitative*, using the term *qualitative* in a title or abstract helps interested readers locate qualitative research. Examples 13.1.1 and 13.1.2 show how some researchers have used the term in titles.

Example 13.1.1

Managing Conflict After Marriages End: A Qualitative Study of Narratives of Ex-Spouses [1]

Example 13.1.2

Factors Affecting Employment Following Spinal Cord Injury: A Qualitative Study [2]

Notice that in both the above titles, the term *qualitative* was used in the subtitles instead of the main titles. This is appropriate because most readers searching for research reports are probably more interested in the variables studied (e.g., "spinal cord injury") than in the methodological approach (i.e., "a qualitative study").

---

[1] Walzer & Oles (2003, p. 192).
[2] Chapin & Kewman (2001, p. 400).

The researcher who wrote the abstract shown in Example 13.1.3 did not use the term "qualitative" in the title, but did use it in the first sentence of the abstract.

Example 13.1.3

This exploratory study examined the identity constructions of African American men using a qualitative research methodology. Seven African American men, ranging in age from 20 to 47 years and whose education levels ranged from a 1st-year university student to a Ph.D., were interviewed for this study. Central to how all of these men defined themselves was the breadwinner or provider role. Participants emphasized education as "insurance" against discrimination and an awareness of educational and occupational opportunities. For these participants, education was a means of ensuring opportunity, which afforded fulfillment of the provider role. This study supports the work of N. Cazenave (1979, 1981), who demonstrated the salience of the provider role among African American men. The implications of the provider role among African American men for research are also discussed. The data also suggested diversity within the African American male experience. As one participant described African American men, "We come like flowers, you know. Some in bouquets, and some wild." By providing constructions of identity that diverge from existing negative stereotypes of African American men, this study attempted to deconstruct those stereotypes. Finally, this study provided a voice to an underrepresented group in the research literature.[3]

Also note that mentioning methods traditionally associated with qualitative research such as "in-depth interviews," "focus groups," and "participant observation" in an abstract will help readers identify the research as qualitative.

This guideline is especially important when qualitative research has been conducted on a topic that has traditionally been approached quantitatively, in which case the use of qualitative methodology on such a topic is a distinguishing characteristic of the research.

➤ Guideline 13.2   Consider discussing the choice of qualitative over quantitative methodology.

A discussion of the choice of qualitative over quantitative methodology is usually placed in the introduction of a research report or in the section on methods. This guideline is especially recommended

---

[3] Diemer (2002, p. 30).

when writing research for an audience that is quantitatively oriented such as readers of a journal that usually publishes quantitative research.

Example 13.2.1 illustrates this guideline. The researchers who wrote it were interested in gaining a better understanding of the lives of preadolescent foster children. The stories that the researchers analyzed were stories the children told in interviews about their lives.

Example 13.2.1

Qualitative approaches are particularly suited to examining the stories of children. Stories reflect a social contextualization of ideas and contain rich content that does not lend itself well to traditional quantitative approaches.... Interviewing children gives this "socially silenced group...[whose] opinions are not heard in the public sphere" an opportunity to have a voice....[4]

Example 13.2.2 also illustrates Guideline 13.2. This is a more elaborate discussion than Example 13.2.1. Longer, detailed discussions of the reasons for choosing qualitative methods are often included in theses and dissertations, but also can be included in term projects and journal articles.

Example 13.2.2

Because the purpose of the current study is to explore mothers' perceptions of the impact of homelessness and shelter life on their relationships with their children, the qualitative research paradigm was selected as most appropriate. Qualitative methodology is particularly useful in studying families because of the emphasis on meanings, interpretations, interactions, and subjective experiences of family members (Daly, 1992; Gilgun, 1992). The theoretical underpinnings of the qualitative research paradigm in family research are phenomenology and symbolic interactionism. Phenomenology attempts to "understand the meaning of events and interactions...and the subjective aspects of people's behavior" (Bogdan & Bicklen, 1992, p. 34). Symbolic interactionism asserts that "human experience is mediated by interpretation.... Objects, people, situations, and events do not possess their own meaning, rather meaning is conferred on them" (Bogdan & Bicklen, 1992, p. 36). Thus, to understand how homelessness and shelter life might impact family relations, it is important to explore the subjective experience of families within the context of homelessness and how mothers interpret and make meaning of that experience.[5]

---

[4] Whiting & Lee (2003, p. 289).
[5] Lindsey (1998, p. 245).

➤ Guideline 13.3 Describe the qualitative method or approach used in the research.

Having stated that the research is qualitative and the reasons for selecting a qualitative approach, it is desirable to describe the particular approach that was used. This is especially important when addressing a quantitatively oriented audience or when using a relatively new qualitative approach. In Example 13.3.1, the researcher indicates the use of a modified grounded theory approach. Note that the paragraph in the example was the first paragraph under the major heading of "Method." Also, note that the researcher provides references where more information on the qualitative method used in the study can be obtained.

Example 13.3.1

An exploratory, modified grounded theory approach to qualitative research was employed in this study. Exploratory or discovery-oriented research methods are purported to be a "necessary first step in the systematic inquiry of a phenomenon, with the goal of describing what is actually happening and then generating hypotheses for future study" (Werstlein & Borders, 1997, p. 122). In the grounded theory tradition, researchers typically conduct interviews during several visits to the field to develop new hypotheses and theory (Creswell, 1998). This approach was modified for the present study in that participants were only interviewed one time. These methods fit well with the major objective of this preliminary study, which was to generate research questions for further study.[6]

➤ Guideline 13.4 Consider "revealing yourself" to your reader.

While quantitative researchers are taught to be "objective" and distance themselves from their research participants to avoid influencing the outcome, qualitative researchers recognize the inherently subjective nature of research. In addition, most qualitative researchers use methods that involve direct interactions between researchers and their participants such as in-depth interviews, participant observation, and focus groups. Because of the interactive nature of much qualitative research, it is sometimes appropriate for researchers to describe themselves when the descriptions are relevant to what is being studied. For instance, the researcher who wrote Example 13.4.1 joined a support group in order to

---

[6] Linton (2003, pp. 216–217).

study the group from the point of view of a participant in the group (i.e., by being a "participant observer"). Because the purpose of the research was to study group support for families with children with mental health needs, the personal revelation in the example is relevant to the research.

Example 13.4.1

The group members and I decided that because I was a family member with psychiatrically ill relatives and had experience with working with groups, a high level of personal involvement with the group's activities was desirable.[7]

➤ Guideline 13.5 Avoid calling a sample "purposive" if it is actually a sample of convenience.

A *purposive* sample is one that is believed to be especially well suited for obtaining meaningful data on a particular research problem. In other words, it is a group of participants that a researcher selects because they have characteristics that make them especially worthy of attention.

When researchers use participants who are selected simply because they are convenient (such as students who happen to be enrolled in a professor's psychology course), the sample should be identified as one of convenience—not purposive—by using a phrase such as "a sample of convenience" or "accidental sample." This is illustrated in Example 13.5.1.

Example 13.5.1

We obtained a convenience sample of 10 families by inviting youth and families from a local Latino after-school program to participate in the study.[8]

➤ Guideline 13.6 If a purposive sample was used, state the basis for selection of participants.

In Example 13.6.1, the researchers purposefully selected cases at the extreme of a distribution.

Example 13.6.1

Because we were interested in exploring factors that support involvement in

---

[7] Mohr (2003, p. 678).
[8] Behnke, Piercy, & Diversi (2004, p. 19).

extracurricular activities, we selected a purposive sample of the most highly involved and competent individuals in childhood to interview about their decisions when they reached adolescence. This sampling procedure is in accordance with Patton's (1990) recommendation for qualitative researchers to purposefully select cases at the extremes of a distribution because they are more likely to contain rich information. Moreover, other scholars have suggested this sampling procedure when examining understudied populations....[9]

➢ Guideline 13.7   Describe how participants were recruited.

Whether a sample of convenience or a purposive sample was used, readers are likely to be interested in how the participants were recruited. This is especially true when studying potentially sensitive issues because poor recruitment procedures may lead to highly atypical samples. Example 13.7.1 shows a portion of a longer, detailed description of the recruitment of divorced individuals in a study of after-marriage conflict. Note that the researchers used a variety of recruitment procedures, which would be expected to result in a more diverse sample than if only one recruitment method had been used.

Example 13.7.1

The sample, from the capital district in upstate New York, was generated through a variety of means. We advertised our study in a local newspaper and used a county clerk's computer listing of people who had filed legal documents as our mailing list for sending outreach letters. We also interviewed people who were legally mandated to attend a class about minimizing negative effects of divorce; to balance these higher conflict participants, we interviewed couples who had voluntarily used mediation.[10]

➢ Guideline 13.8   Provide demographic information.

Demographics (i.e., background variables) help readers "see" the participants. While a variety of statistics may be used to summarize demographic data (e.g., means and standard deviations), sometimes it is possible to provide demographics by using some simple numbers, which is illustrated in Example 13.8.1.

---

[9] Fredricks et al. (2002, p. 72).
[10] Walzer & Oles (2003, p. 193).

Example 13.8.1

There were 13 men and 12 women in our sample. The age range of the participants interviewed was 29 to 68. Most of the participants were White; one person self-identified as Latina and another as Native American. The sample was primarily working-class and middle-class, although 2 women had very little income and 2 men were quite wealthy.[11]

➢ Guideline 13.9   Provide specific information on data collection methods.

In an interview study, it is insufficient to state merely that "in-depth, semistructured interviews were conducted." Readers will want to know how the initial questions were developed as well as the topics these questions were meant to cover. Example 13.9.1 illustrates this.

Example 13.9.1

An interview format was selected due to the depth of data it can offer and its ability to reveal participants' own perspectives on their experiences. The semistructured nature of the interview protocol allowed for exploratory probing and further questioning when necessary. The interview questions explored family functioning, reasons for immigration, and experiences in the United States, especially with regard to school, family, and peers. There were also questions about mental health concerns and coping as related to immigration.

The interview protocol was developed after performing an extensive review of the literature. The questions were primarily based on the research on cultural adjustment (Rosenthal & Feldman, 1990, 1996; Padilla et al., 1985) and acculturation.... Questions were designed specifically for Asian immigrant youth. Interviewers were encouraged to probe further if there were any ambiguities in participants' responses.[12]

Note that it may not be necessary to state the actual questions used, especially if the wording of the questions varied somewhat from participant to participant and the content of the questions changed over the course of a qualitative study in light of the data collected from earlier participants. On the other hand, if there are key questions that were asked of all participants, consider including them in the research report. If there are many questions, either provide just a sample for each domain of interest or provide them all in a table or appendix. In Example 13.9.2, the researchers describe the areas covered by the questions and then refer the

---

[11] Walzer & Oles (2003, p. 193).
[12] Yeh et al. (2003, p. 486).

readers to a table that contains 17 key questions (e.g., "Will you tell me about a time when your child had difficulty breathing during the night?") organized under six topics (e.g., "Family response to asthma"). Also, note these desirable characteristics of Example 13.9.2: (a) the researchers identify the individual who conducted the interviews, (b) the researchers state when and where the interviews were conducted, and (c) the researchers indicate the basis for developing the interview guide.

Example 13.9.2

The primary author interviewed families three times in their homes for 3–6 months after the hospitalization of their child. The home was chosen as the most convenient and relaxed setting for parents of young children. The interview guide was modified for this study from an interview guide used by Chesla (1988) in her study of families coping with chronic illness in children. Parents were asked to describe how they evaluated symptoms [of asthma], assessed severity, managed compromised breathing in young children, took the step of seeking emergency care, and responded during hospitalization. [Seventeen] key interview questions are presented in Table 3.[13]

Providing details on data collection is also desirable when reporting on observational studies. Consider answering questions such as these when writing the description: Was the observer a participant or nonparticipant? When were the observations made? How often were they made? How were the data recorded? For what types of behaviors did the researcher initially look? What types of changes took place in the data collection method as the collection of data proceeded?

➤ Guideline 13.10   Describe steps taken to ensure the trustworthiness of the data.

Qualitative researchers use a variety of methods to ensure that their data is trustworthy. These should be described in enough detail to reassure readers that the data are not merely the reflection of one researcher's personal opinions. For instance, when "member checks" are used, describe how the activity was conducted and by whom, as illustrated in Example 13.10.1.

Example 13.10.1

Before proceeding with the analysis of the focus group data, the major themes

---

[13] Koenig & Chesla (2004, pp. 59–60).

identified by the researchers as well as the examples selected to support the themes were presented in writing to a sample of 10 of the 20 participants. Although all 20 were invited to participate in this phase of the research, only 10 were available at the appointed time for this activity. The first stage of the member check was to have the ten participants highlight with a marker those themes and examples that they deemed most important. They were also asked to cross out any that seemed to be off track or unrepresentative of their understandings of the members' meanings in the focus groups. The second stage was to hold two small-group meetings with five participants each to discuss the material they highlighted and crossed out. This activity was conducted by....

Likewise, if "triangulation of data sources" was used to ensure trustworthiness, describe what each source was (e.g., parents, children, and teachers) and specifically how the data were collected from each source. Also, if "triangulation of methods of data collection" was used (e.g., interviews as well as observations), describe each clearly.

As a general rule, the methods used to ensure trustworthiness, including others not mentioned here, should not be simply referred to in a research report. Instead, they should be described in some detail.

➤ Guideline 13.11   Provide a specific description of the method of analysis.

A variety of methods have been proposed for the analysis of information gathered through qualitative research. It is usually desirable to not only name the method(s) used, but to describe how they are applied. Such information helps readers understand how the researchers approached the analysis.

The researchers who wrote Example 13.11.1 used multiple data analysis methods, which is often desirable. The example shows their description of one of them (i.e., the "constant comparative approach"). Note that they provide a reference where readers can obtain more information on this approach. Providing such references is also desirable.

Example 13.11.1

Multiple data analysis tactics were applied. [A] pervasive method of analysis was the constant comparative approach (Glaser & Strauss, 1967). This method consists of going back and forth from the data to the display of words and concepts, constantly checking and revising, if needed. Basic to the method was reading and rereading the data, immersing in the data, incubating time to think and reflect, verifying themes that occurred over time, and re-examining conditions, context, and consequences presented in the data, thus confirming subthemes (Glaser and Strauss). Other methods included....[14]

➤ Guideline 13.12   If two or more researchers participated in analyzing the data, describe how they arrived at a consensus.

One specific technique often used in qualitative research is to have two or more individuals participate in the analysis of the data. When this is done, readers will be interested in knowing about the extent to which these individuals were in agreement. Questions that might be addressed in light of this guideline are: Did the researchers analyze the data independently and then confer, or did they analyze it together from the beginning? If there were disagreements on some aspects of the interpretation, how were they resolved? How confident does each researcher feel in the final interpretations presented in the report?

➤ Guideline 13.13   In the results section of a qualitative report, provide quantitative results on quantitative matters.

Conducting qualitative research does not preclude the use of statistics when they are appropriate. Some matters naturally lend themselves to quantification. Note that the term "many" in Example 13.13.1 is a quantitative term because it clearly implies that some number had their heads down. Yet, "many" is unnecessarily vague if the researcher knows how many students or what percentage of students did this. The improved version is consistent with this guideline.

Example 13.13.1

Many of the students were observed to have their heads down on their desks during the mathematics lesson.

Improved Version of Example 13.13.1

About 25% of the students were observed to have their heads down on their desks during the mathematics lesson.

---

[14] Colvin, Chenoweth, Bold, & Harding (2004, pp. 51–52).

In short, just because the main analysis in a qualitative research project is nonquantitative does not rule out the use of statistics when they are appropriate for other purposes in a report on qualitative research.

➢ Guideline 13.14   Consider using the major themes as subheadings in the results section.

Often, the results of qualitative research are described in terms of major and minor themes. If the results section of a report on qualitative research is long, consider using the names of the major themes as subheadings in the results section. This will help your readers understand your results. In a report on women who had Hepatitis C, the authors of Example 13.14.1 used the themes shown as subheadings.

Example 13.14.1

Major themes used as subheadings (in bold) in the results section:
Seeking a diagnosis
   Our respondents' encounter with Hepatitis C began in 1977, some 12 years before the virus was....
Constructing alternative explanations
   When mainstream medicine failed to identify a reason for their ill health, individual women constructed various kinds of explanations....
Labile emotional reactions to the diagnosis
   Initially, participants were relieved, as the following excerpts illustrate....
Concern about emerging dysfunction
   Cognitive dysfunction in terms of failures of concentration, memory loss, difficulty in comprehending....
Progressive erosion of existing and expected roles
   Role erosion emerged from the impact on everyday activities of the physical limitations that the women....
Negative impact on familial and other close relationships
   The women's descriptions of the impact of their condition on relationships fell into four categories....
[Author's note: *There were four subheadings for minor themes under **Negative impact on familial and other close relationships**. They are*: **Social life with and within the family, Effect on partners, Effect on children, Effect on relatives and friends.**][15]

---

[15] Dunne & Quayle (2001, pp. 682–689).

➢ Guideline 13.15   If quotations are reported, consider stating the basis for their selection.

In qualitative research, large amounts of narrative material (the raw data) are often collected. Readers will be interested in learning the basis for your selection of the limited number of quotations presented in the results section of a research report. Note that there may be different reasons for the selection of various quotations. Some might be selected because they are the most articulate expressions of a recurring theme. Others might be selected because they are the most emotional. Still others might be presented to illustrate a typical response to some issue.

The most common basis for selecting quotations is that they are somehow "typical" or "representative." When making this claim about quotations, consider indicating *how* typical they are by indicating the number of participants who expressed similar sentiments. Example 13.15.1 illustrates this.

Example 13.15.1

Results are presented in terms of the number of cases (participants) in each domain/category (see Table 1). We described a category as *general* if it applied to all 8 participants, *typical* if it applied to 4–7 participants, and *variant* if it applied to 2–3 participants. Categories that applied to only 1 participant were dropped.[16]

[Author's note: Only one of the nine domains and only two of the 37 categories in the original table are shown here.]

Table 1
Domains and Categories of Responses

Domain	Category
Family	A. Family problems were denied (typical; $n = 4$)
	B. Participant's mother has difficulty with English (variant; $n = 3$)

Note that Example 13.15.1 is taken out of context from a report in which the meanings of the categories and quotations are discussed and interpreted in some detail. The results section of a qualitative report should *not* consist merely of a listing of categories and the associated percentages or numbers of cases. Instead, they should be interpreted and discussed in terms of the points they illustrate and the meanings attached to them by the researchers and participants.

---

[16] Yeh et al. (2003, pp. 487–489).

➢ Guideline 13.16   Consider discussing alternative interpretations of the data and why they were rejected.

If there are obvious alternative interpretations, explicitly discuss the reasons for rejecting them. For instance, a researcher might use quotations or talk about trends in the data that run counter to the alternatives, which would help explain why one interpretation was selected over another.

Concluding Comments

Writing effective reports of both qualitative and quantitative research is an art that can be mastered only with practice and careful modeling of the writing of skilled professionals. To move beyond this book and become a master of empirical research writing, the most important thing you can do is read numerous examples of the research written by others—with attention to detail, style, and mechanics. Skimming articles or, worse yet, reading only the abstracts is not sufficient. Instead, you should read research reports in their entirety while evaluating them by asking questions such as: What makes a report effective or ineffective? At what points did you get lost while reading a report? What else could the researcher have done to assist you in following his or her line of reasoning? In short, by becoming a critical consumer of research written by others, you will become a skilled writer of empirical research reports.

Exercise for Chapter 13

PART A

1. According to this chapter, is it more appropriate to put the term "qualitative" in a subtitle *or* to put it in the main title? Explain.

2. According to this chapter, when is it especially important to discuss the choice of qualitative methods over quantitative methods in a research report?

3. Because qualitative research often involves direct interactions, what should researchers consider describing?

4. How is a "purposive sample" defined in this chapter?

5. When should researchers refer to their sample as a "sample of convenience"?

6. According to this chapter, is it necessary to use elaborate statistics to present demographic information?

7. According to this chapter, methods used to ensure trustworthiness should not be simply referred to in a research report. Instead, what should be done?

8. If two or more researchers participated in analyzing the data, what should be described in the research report?

9. Is it ever desirable to report quantities in the results section of a report on qualitative research?

10. According to this chapter, what is the most common basis for selecting quotations from participants to include in a report on qualitative research?

11. Should alternative interpretations of the data be discussed in a qualitative research report?

PART B: Locate a report on qualitative research that you think illustrates many of the guidelines in this chapter. Bring it to class for discussion.

Chapter 14

Preparing a Reference List[1]

The reference list is usually the last element in a research report.[2] It begins with the word "References" as its heading.

In the social and behavioral sciences, the most popular method for citing references is the Harvard method, which is also known as the "author–date method." As you know from Guideline 6.19 in Chapter 6, the author's last name and year of publication can be made the noun of a sentence, as in: Doe (2004) reported that X is larger than Z. The name and year can also be made parenthetical to a sentence, as in: X has been reported as being larger than Z (Doe, 2004).

Researchers usually cite mainly journal articles in their research reports because journal articles are the major source of primary (i.e., original) reports of the research of others. Thus, this chapter emphasizes the preparation of a reference list that refers to journal articles. For details on referencing other types of sources, consult a style manual (see Guideline 14.1).

➢ Guideline 14.1   Select a style manual and carefully follow its directions for preparing a reference list.

A style manual specifies mechanical features such as spacing, margins, levels of heading, as well as the preparation of reference lists for manuscripts written for a particular audience. For instance, the *Publication Manual of the American Psychological Association* prescribes mechanics for the preparation of manuscripts for publication in the journals published by the Association. Because of its comprehensive nature, it is also the style manual for many journals in other fields such as education, sociology, nursing, and physical education.

It is important to notice and pay attention to the details in a style manual because some matters are a matter of preference, which can be

---

[1] Portions of this chapter were adopted with permission from Pan (2004).

[2] If there are appendices to a research report, these should be included after the reference list.

handled in a number of different ways. Example 14.1.1 shows a reference list entry for a journal article formatted in American Psychological Association (APA) style. Notice that many of the details of the style cannot be derived from intuition. For instance, the first and middle names of authors are not spelled out and the "&" sign, not the word "and," is used when there are multiple authors. Likewise, APA style does not use the abbreviation "pp." before the page numbers (165–177). People familiar with this style know that the numbers at the end of the reference must be the page numbers because the style manual says that they should be the last element.

Example 14.1.1

Schleicher, D. J., Watt, J. D., & Greguras, G. J. (2004). Reexamining the job satisfaction–performance relationship: The complexity of attitudes. *Journal of Applied Psychology, 89*, 165–177.

Notice the use of a *hanging indent* (i.e., the first line is not indented but the subsequent lines in the reference are indented) in Example 14.1.1. The hanging indent makes the authors' names stand out in a reference list (examine the reference list after this chapter). In Microsoft Word, a hanging indent can be easily created by clicking on "Format," then "Paragraph," which will default to the "Indents and Spacing" dialog box. To reveal the word "Hanging," click on the down arrow under the word "Special." Then click on the word "Hanging" to create a hanging indent.

➤ Guideline 14.2   A journal title is treated like a book title; either underline or italicize it.

Traditional academic libraries usually collect all the issues of a journal for a year and have them case bound (i.e., put into a hardback cover). This results in a "book" for each year of the journal. As you learned in freshman English, underline the titles of books, and, in this case, journal titles.

Because most typewriters do not have the capability of producing italics, underlining is used to tell a typesetter to italicize what is underlined. With modern word processors, however, italicizing words is quite easy. If you are writing a research report for a class using a word processing program, check with your instructor to determine whether you should italicize or underline the titles of journal articles.

➤ Guideline 14.3   While volume numbers are important in identifying a journal article, issue numbers are not.

Certain conventions in numbering journals are almost always followed. For instance, each issue of a journal has an issue number, almost always starting with "1" for the first issue of a year, followed by "2" for the second issue of a year, and so on. All issues within a year have a volume number. Thus, the volume number *66* (italicized) in Example 14.3.1 indicates that the reference is in the volume published in the 66th year of the journal's existence.

Example 14.3.1

Martino, S. C., Collins, R. L., & Ellickson, P. L. (2004). Substance use and early marriage. *Journal of Marriage and the Family, 66,* 244–257.

Within each volume, page numbers are consecutive. Thus, the first issue of a journal for a year begins with page 1. If that issue ends on page 223, then the next issue for the same year begins with page 224. Thus, when all issues for a year (i.e., the volume) are case bound by a library, each page in a volume has a unique number. As a result, when you are looking for an article in the library, you can pick up the volume of interest, which will be numbered on the spine of the volume, and turn to the pages of the article. It is not necessary to look for a particular issue number. Hence, many journals have authors omit issue numbers in their reference lists.

➤ Guideline 14.4   Double-check punctuation in accordance with the style manual.

A style manual will specify the punctuation to be used in a reference list. For instance, if the style manual being used shows a period mark at the close of the parentheses containing the year of publication, be careful not to substitute a comma.

➤ Guideline 14.5   Double-check capitalization in accordance with the style manual.

In APA style, for instance, only the first letter of the first word in the main title and in the subtitle of the article begins with capital letters.

Capping the letters of all major words in the title in a reference list is not APA style and could cost points when a research paper is graded.[3]

➢ Guideline 14.6   A reference list should contain entries only for those that have been cited in the research report.

Do not treat the reference list as a suggested reading list. Include only those that were actually cited in the body of the research report.

➢ Guideline 14.7   Cross-check reference citations in the body of the report with those in the reference list.

Examine each citation in the body of the research report and check to see that (a) it is included in the reference list, (b) names are spelled the same in both places, and (c) years of publication are the same.

Exercise for Chapter 14

1. What is missing from the following reference?

   Jones, B. F., & Smith, A. D. (2004). The relationship between job satisfaction and income level. *Journal of Labor*, 14–20.

2. What is missing from the following reference?

   Jones, B. F., Smith, A. D. (2004). The relationship between job satisfaction and income level. *Journal of Labor*, *35*, 14–20.

3. Are italics used appropriately in the following reference? Explain.

   Jones, B. F., & Smith, A. D. (2004). *The relationship between job satisfaction and income level.* Journal of Labor, 35, 14–20.

---

[3] This guideline only applies to the reference list. The first letters of all major words in the title of a research report (i.e., the title that appears at the beginning of the report) should be capitalized.

4. What should be deleted from the following reference?

   Jones, B. F., & Smith, A. D. (2004). The relationship between job satisfaction and income level. *Journal of Labor, 35,* pp. 14–20.

5. What should be changed in the following reference?

   Jones, Bernard F., & Smith, Amy D. (2004). The relationship between job satisfaction and income level. *Journal of Labor, 35,* 14–20.

6. What is wrong with the punctuation in the following reference?

   Jones, B. F., & Smith, A. D. (2004), The relationship between job satisfaction and income level. *Journal of Labor, 35,* 14–20.

7. What is wrong with the capitalization in the following reference?

   Jones, B. F., & Smith, A. D. (2004). The Relationship Between Job Satisfaction and Income Level. *Journal of Labor, 35,* 14–20.

Notes:

References

Abela, J. R. Z., & Sullivan, C. (2003). A test of Beck's cognitive diathesis-stress theory of depression in early adolescents. *Journal of Early Adolescence, 23*, 384–404.

Altman, J. C. (2003). A qualitative examination of client participation in agency-initiated services. *Families in Society: The Journal of Contemporary Human Service, 84*, 471–479.

Babcock, J. C., & Steiner, R. (1999). The relationship between treatment, incarceration, and recidivism of battering: A program evaluation of Seattle's coordinated community response to domestic violence. *Journal of Family Psychology, 13*, 46–59.

Bakari, R. (2003). Preservice teachers' attitudes toward teaching African American students: Contemporary research. *Urban Education, 38*, 640–654.

Bauer, K. W., Yang, Y. W., & Austin, S. B. (2004). "How can we stay healthy when you're throwing all of this in front of us?" Findings from focus groups and interviews in middle schools on environmental influences on nutrition and physical activity. *Health Education & Behavior, 31*, 34–46.

Behnke, A. O., Piercy, K. W., & Diversi, M. (2004). Educational and occupational aspirations of Latino youth and their parents. *Hispanic Journal of Behavioral Sciences, 26*, 16–35.

Buchko, K. J., & Witzig, T. F., Jr. (2003). Relationship between God-image and religious behaviors. *Psychological Reports, 93*, 1141–1148.

Buckner, J. C., Bassuk, E. L., Weinreb, L. F., & Brooks, M. G. (1999). Homelessness and its relation to the mental health and behavior of low-income school-age children. *Developmental Psychology, 35*, 246–257.

Bushman, B. J., & Bonacci, A. M. (2002). Violence and sex impair memory for television ads. *Journal of Applied Psychology, 87*, 557–564.

Caetano, R., Ramisetty-Mikler, S., & McGrath, C. (2004). Acculturation, drinking, and intimate partner violence among Hispanic couples in the United States: A longitudinal study. *Hispanic Journal of Behavioral Science, 26*, 60–78.

Chapin, M. H., & Kewman, D. G. (2001). Factors affecting employment following spinal cord injury: A qualitative study. *Rehabilitation Psychology, 46*, 400–416.

Colvin, J., Chenoweth, L., Bold, M., & Harding, C. (2004). Caregivers of older adults: Advantages and disadvantages of Internet-based social support. *Family Relations, 53*, 49–57.

Diemer, M. A. (2002). Constructions of provider identity among African American men: An exploratory study. *Cultural Diversity and Ethnic Minority Psychology, 8*, 30–40.

Dunne, E. A., & Quayle, E. (2001). The impact of Iatrogenically acquired Hepatitis C infection on the well-being and relationships of a group of Irish women. *Journal of Health Psychology, 6*, 679–692.

Eisenberg, A. R. (2002). Maternal teaching talk within families of Mexican descent: Influences of task and socioeconomic status. *Hispanic Journal of Behavioral Sciences, 24*, 206–224.

Fitzgerald, J. (2001). Can minimally trained college student volunteers help young at-risk children to read better? *Reading Research Quarterly, 36*, 28–47.

Fredricks, J. A., Alfeld-Liro, C., Hruda, L. Z., Eccles, J. S., Patrick, H., & Ryan, A. M. (2002). A qualitative exploration of adolescents' commitment to athletics and the arts. *Journal of Adolescent Research, 17*, 68–97.

Glass, C. S. (2001). Factors influencing teaching strategies used with children who display attention deficit hyperactivity disorder. *Education, 122*, 70–79.

Golden, C., Golden, C. J., & Schneider, B. (2003). Cell phone use and visual attention. *Perceptual and Motor Skills, 97*, 385–389.

Graham, S., & Juvonen, J. (2002). Ethnicity, peer harassment, and adjustment in middle school: An exploratory study. *Journal of Early Adolescence, 22*, 173–199.

Hamid, P. N., Yue, X. D., & Leung, C. M. (2003). Adolescent coping in different Chinese family environments. *Adolescence, 38*, 111–130.

Hill, C. E., & Kellems, I. S. (2002). Development and use of the helping skills measure to assess client perceptions of the effects of training and of helping skills in sessions. *Journal of Counseling Psychology, 49*, 264–272.

Hirokawa, K., Dohi, I., Vannieuwenhuyse, B., & Miyata, Y. (2001). Comparison of French and Japanese individuals with reference to Hofstede's concepts of individualism and masculinity. *Psychological Reports, 89*, 243–251.

Holsen, I., Kraft, P., & Røysamb, E. (2001). The relationship between body image and depressed mood in adolescence: A 5-year longitudinal study. *Journal of Health Psychology, 6*, 613–637.

Hudson, A., Kirksey, K., & Holzemer, W. (2004). The influence of symptoms on quality of life among HIV-infected women. *Western Journal of Nursing Research, 26*, 9–23.

Hughes, R. B., Nosek, M. A., Howland, C. A., Groff, J. Y., & Mullen, P. D. (2003). Health promotion for women with physical disabilities: A pilot study. *Rehabilitation Psychology, 48*, 182–188.

Johnstone, K. M., Ashbaugh, H., & Warfield, T. D. (2002). Effects of repeated practice and contextual-writing experiences on college students' writing skills. *Journal of Educational Psychology, 94*, 305–315.

Koenig, K., & Chesla, C. A. (2004). Asthma management among low-income Latino and African American families of infants and young children. *Family Relations, 53*, 58–67.

Kulis, S., Marsiglia, F. F., & Hecht, M. L. (2002). Gender labels and gender identity as predictors of drug use among ethnically diverse middle school students. *Youth & Society, 33*, 442–474.

Larsen, J. T., McGraw, A. P., & Cacioppo, J. T. (2001). Can people feel happy and sad at the same time? *Journal of Personality and Social Psychology, 81*, 684–696.

Lightsey, O. W., & Hulsey, C. D. (2002). Impulsivity, coping, stress, and problem gambling among university students. *Journal of Counseling Psychology, 49*, 202–211.

Lindsey, E. W. (1998). The impact of homelessness and shelter life on family relationships. *Family Relations, 47*, 243–252.

Linton, J. M. (2003). A preliminary qualitative investigation of group processes in group supervision: Perspectives of master's level practicum students. *Journal for Specialists in Group Work, 28*, 215–226.

Lowis, M. J., & Mooney, S. (2001). Examination performance and graphological analysis of students' handwriting. *Perceptual and Motor Skills, 93*, 367–381.

Martino, S. C., Collins, R. L., & Ellickson, P. L. (2004). Substance use and early marriage. *Journal of Marriage and Family, 66*, 244–257.

Mason, W. A., & Windle, M. (2002). A longitudinal study of the effects of religiosity on adolescent alcohol use and alcohol-related problems. *Journal of Adolescent Research, 17*, 346–363.

Matsui, T., Kakuyama, T., & Tsuzuki, Y. (2003). Effects of situational conditions on students' views of business ethics. *Psychological Reports, 93*, 1135–1140.

McCreary, D. R., & Sadava, S. W. (2001). Gender differences in relationships among perceived attractiveness, life satisfaction, and health in adults as a function of body mass index and perceived weight. *Psychology of Men and Masculinity, 2*, 108–116.

McDonald, D. D., Deloge, J. A., Joslin, N., Petow, W. A., Severson, J. S., Votino, R., Shea, M. D., Drenga, J. M. L., Brennan, M. T., Moran, A. B., & Del Signore, E. (2003). Communicating end-of-life preferences. *Western Journal of Nursing Research, 25*, 652–666.

References

McMahon, B. T., West, S. L., Lewis, A. N., Armstrong, A. J., & Conway, J. P. (2004). Hate crimes and disability in America. *Rehabilitation Counseling Bulletin, 47,* 66–75.

Mohr, W. K. (2003). The substance of a support group. *Western Journal of Nursing Research, 25,* 676–692.

Muraven, M., Collins, R. L., & Nienhaus, K. (2002). Self-control and alcohol restraint: An initial application of the self-control strength model. *Psychology of Addictive Behaviors, 16,* 113–120.

O'Connell, K. A., Gerkovich, M. M., Bott, M. J., Cook, M. R., & Shiffman, S. (2002). The effect of anticipatory strategies on the first day of smoking cessation. *Psychology of Addictive Behaviors, 16,* 50–156.

Pan, M. L. (2004). *Preparing Literature Reviews: Qualitative and Quantitative Approaches* (2nd ed.). Glendale, CA: Pyrczak Publishing.

Parks, C. A., Hesselbrock, M. N., Hesselbrock, V. M., & Segal, B. (2003). Factors affecting entry into substance abuse treatment: Gender differences among alcohol-dependent Alaska Natives. *Social Work Research, 27,* 151–161.

Penno, J. F., Wilkinson, I. A. G., & Moore, D. W. (2002). Vocabulary acquisition from teacher explanation and repeated listening to stories: Do they overcome the Matthew Effect? *Journal of Educational Psychology, 94,* 23–33.

Ramanaiah, N. V., Rielage, J. K., & Sharpe, J. P. (2001). Spiritual well-being and personality. *Psychological Reports, 89,* 659–662.

Reese, R. J., Conoley, C. W., & Brossart, D. F. (2002). Effectiveness of Telephone Counseling: A Field-Based Investigation. *Journal of Counseling Psychology, 49,* 233–242.

Rice, K. G., Cunningham, T. J., & Young, M. B. (1997). Attachment to parents, social competence, and emotional well-being: A comparison of Black and White late adolescents. *Journal of Counseling Psychology, 44,* 89–101.

Schleicher, D. J., Watt, J. D., & Greguras, G. J. (2004). Reexamining the job satisfaction–performance relationship: The complexity of attitudes. *Journal of Applied Psychology, 89,* 165–177.

Schneider, M. E., & Ward, D. J. (2003). The role of ethnic identification and perceived social support in Latinos' adjustment to college. *Hispanic Journal of Behavioral Sciences, 25,* 539–554.

Schumm, W. R., Bell, D. B., & Resnick, G. (2001). Recent research on family factors and readiness: Implications for military leaders. *Psychological Reports, 89,* 153–165.

Schwartz, A. E., McRoy, R. G., & Downs, A. C. (2004). Adolescent mothers in a transitional living facility: An exploratory study of support networks and attachment patterns. *Journal of Adolescent Research, 19,* 85–112.

Shadel, W. G., Niaura, R., and Abrams, D. B. (2002). Adolescents' reactions to the imagery displayed in smoking and antismoking advertisements. *Psychology of Addictive Behaviors, 16,* 173–176.

Strom, R., Dohrmann, J., Strom, P., Griswold, D., Beckert, T., Strom, S., Moore, E., & Nakagawa, K. (2002). African American mothers of early adolescents: Perceptions of two generations. *Youth and Society, 33,* 394–417.

Thiede, H., Valleroy, L. A., MacKellar, D. A., Celentano, D. D., Ford, W. L., Hagan, H., Koblin, B. A., LaLota, M., McFarland, W., Shehan, D. A., & Torian, L. V. (2003). Regional patterns and correlates of substance use among young men who have sex with men in seven US urban areas. *American Journal of Public Health, 93,* 1915–1921.

Toselli, M., Farneti, P., & Grossi, E. (2001). Role of motor imitation in traversability of surfaces by walking infants. *Perceptual and Motor Skills, 93,* 523–530.

Umaña-Taylor, A. J., & Bámaca-Gómez, M. Y. (2003). Generational differences in resistance to peer pressure among Mexican-origin adolescents. *Youth & Society, 35,* 183–203.

Walker, K. L., & Dixon, V. (2002). Spirituality and academic performance among African American college students. *The Journal of Black Psychology, 28,* 107–121.

Wallace, J. M., Forman, T. A., Caldwell, C. H., & Willis, D. S. (2003). Religion and U.S. secondary school students: Current patterns, recent trends, and sociodemographic correlates. *Youth & Society, 35,* 98–125.

Walzer, S., & Oles, T. P. (2003). Managing conflict after marriages end: A qualitative study of narratives of ex-spouses. *Families in Society: The Journal of Contemporary Human Services, 84,* 192–200.

Whiting, J. B., & Lee, R. E., III. (2003). Voices from the system: A qualitative study of foster children's stories. *Family Relations, 52,* 288–295.

Wiggins, M. S. (2002). Psychophysiological comparison of self-efficacy and resting heart rate. *Perceptual and Motor Skills, 94,* 720–722.

Williams, R., Doctor, J., Patterson, D., & Gibran, N. (2003). Health outcomes for burn survivors: A 2-year follow-up. *Rehabilitation Psychology, 48,* 189–194.

Yeh, C. J., Arora, A. K., Inose, M., Okubo, Y., Li, R. H., & Greene, P. (2003). The cultural adjustment and mental health of Japanese immigrant youth. *Adolescence, 38,* 481–500.

Yip, K., Ngan, M., & Lam, I. (2003). A qualitative study of parental influence on and response to adolescents' self-cutting in Hong Kong. *Families in Society: The Journal of Contemporary Human Services, 84,* 405–416.

Appendix A

Checklist of Guidelines

Instructors may wish to refer to the following checklist numbers when commenting on students' papers (e.g., "See Guideline 5.2"). Students can use this checklist to review important points as they prepare their research reports and proposals.

Chapter 1 Structuring a Research Report

____ 1.1 A research report typically has a brief title.

____ 1.2 An abstract usually follows the title.

____ 1.3 The body of a basic research report should have an introduction that includes a literature review, a section on research methods, a section on results, and a discussion.

____ 1.4 The section on research methods almost always has two main subsections: "Participants" and "Instrumentation."

____ 1.5 Be generous in using subheadings within each main section of the report.

____ 1.6 In a thesis or dissertation, the introduction and the literature review are often presented in separate chapters.

Chapter 2 Writing Simple Research Hypotheses

____ 2.1 A simple research hypothesis should name two variables and indicate the type of relationship expected between them.

____ 2.2 When there is an independent variable, name a specific dependent variable.

____ 2.3 When a relationship is expected only in a particular population, consider naming the population in the hypothesis.

____ 2.4 A simple hypothesis should be as specific as possible, yet expressed in a single sentence.

____ 2.5 If a comparison is to be made, the elements to be compared should be stated.

____ 2.6 Because most hypotheses deal with the behavior of groups, plural forms should usually be used.

____ 2.7 Avoid sex-role stereotypes in the statement of a hypothesis.

____ 2.8 A hypothesis should be free of terms and phrases that do not add to its meaning.

____ 2.9 A hypothesis should indicate what will actually be studied—not the possible implications of a study or value judgments of the author.

___ 2.10 A hypothesis usually should name variables in the order in which they occur or will be measured.

___ 2.11 Avoid using the words "significant" or "significance" in a hypothesis.

___ 2.12 Avoid using the word "prove" in a hypothesis.

___ 2.13 Avoid using two different terms to refer to the same variable in a hypothesis.

___ 2.14 Avoid making precise statistical predictions in a hypothesis.

Chapter 3 A Closer Look at Hypotheses

___ 3.1 A "statement of the hypothesis" may contain more than one hypothesis. It is permissible to include them in a single sentence as long as the sentence is reasonably concise and its meaning is clear.

___ 3.2 When a number of related hypotheses are to be stated, consider presenting them in a numbered or lettered list.

___ 3.3 The hypothesis or hypotheses should be placed before the section on methods.

___ 3.4 It is permissible to use terms other than the term "hypothesis" to refer to a hypothesis.

___ 3.5 In a research report, a hypothesis should flow from the narrative that immediately precedes it.

___ 3.6 A hypothesis may be stated without indicating the type of relationship expected between variables. To qualify as a hypothesis, however, it must specify that some unknown type of relationship is expected.

___ 3.7 When a researcher has a research hypothesis, it should be stated in the research report; the null hypothesis need not always be stated.

Chapter 4 Writing Research Purposes, Objectives, and Questions

___ 4.1 If you will be conducting *qualitative* research, consider writing a research purpose or question instead of a hypothesis.

___ 4.2 When the goal of research is to describe one or more groups without describing relationships among variables, write a research purpose or question instead of a hypothesis.

___ 4.3 When there is insufficient evidence to permit formulation of a hypothesis regarding a relationship between variables, write a research purpose or question.

___ 4.4 When writing a research question, avoid writing a question that implies that the data will lead to a simple "yes" or "no" answer.

___ 4.5 The research purpose or question should be as specific as possible, yet stated concisely.

___ 4.6 When stating related purposes or questions, consider presenting them in a numbered or lettered list.

___ 4.7 In a research report, a research purpose or question should flow from the narrative that immediately precedes it.

Chapter 5 Writing Titles

____ 5.1 If only a small number of variables is studied, the title should name the variables.

____ 5.2 If many variables are studied, only the *types* of variables should be named.

____ 5.3 The title of a journal article should be concise; the title of a thesis or dissertation may be longer.

____ 5.4 A title should indicate what was studied—not the results or conclusions of the study.

____ 5.5 Consider mentioning the population(s) in a title when a study is deliberately delimited to a particular type of population.

—— 5.6 Consider the use of subtitles to amplify the purposes or methods of study.

—— 5.7 If a study is strongly tied to a particular model or theory, consider mentioning it in the title.

____ 5.8 A title may be in the form of a question; this form should be used sparingly and with caution.

____ 5.9 In titles, use the words "effect" and "influence" with caution.

____ 5.10 A title should be consistent with the research hypothesis, purpose, or question.

____ 5.11 Consider mentioning unique features of a study in its title.

____ 5.12 Avoid clever titles, especially if they fail to communicate important information about the report.

Chapter 6 Writing Introductions and Literature Reviews

____ 6.1 Start the introduction by describing the problem area; gradually shift its focus to specific research hypotheses, purposes, or questions.

____ 6.2 Start long introductions and literature reviews with a paragraph that describes their organization, and use subheadings to guide readers.

____ 6.3 The importance of a topic should be explicitly stated in the introduction.

____ 6.4 A statement on the importance of a topic should be specific to the topic investigated.

____ 6.5 Consider pointing out the number or percentage of people who are affected by the problem you are studying.

____ 6.6 The literature review should be presented in the form of an essay—not in the form of an annotated list.

____ 6.7 Avoid using long strings of reference citations for a single finding or theory.

____ 6.8 Discuss theories that have relevance to the research.

____ 6.9 The literature review should emphasize the findings of previous research—not just the research methodologies and names of variables studied.

____ 6.10 Feel free to express opinions about the quality and importance of the research being cited.

____ 6.11 Point out trends and themes in the literature.

___ 6.12 Point out gaps in the literature.

___ 6.13 Point out how the current study differs from previous studies.

___ 6.14 Peripheral research may be cited in a thesis or dissertation when no literature with a direct bearing on the research topic can be located.

___ 6.15 Use direct quotations sparingly in literature reviews.

___ 6.16 Report sparingly on the details of the literature being cited.

___ 6.17 Consider using literature to provide the historical context for the present study.

___ 6.18 Consider citing prior literature reviews on your topic.

___ 6.19 When using the Harvard method for citing references, decide whether to emphasize the authorship or the content of each reference.

___ 6.20 Avoid referring to the credentials and affiliations of the authors of the literature that is reviewed.

___ 6.21 Use of the first person is acceptable if used sparingly to refer to personal observations, experiences, and beliefs.

Chapter 7 Writing Definitions

___ 7.1 All variables in a research hypothesis, purpose, or question should be defined.

___ 7.2 The definitions of defining attributes of a population (also called "control variables") should be specific.

___ 7.3 Theories and models on which the research is based should be defined.

___ 7.4 Conceptual definitions should be specific.

___ 7.5 Operational definitions should be provided, usually in the method section of a report.

___ 7.6 For each conceptual definition, there should be a corresponding operational definition.

___ 7.7 If a published instrument was used, the variable measured by it may be operationally defined by citing the reference for the instrument.

___ 7.8 If an unpublished instrument was used, consider reproducing sample questions or the entire instrument in the report.

___ 7.9 Operational definitions should be sufficiently specific so that another researcher can replicate the study.

___ 7.10 Even a highly operational definition may not be a useful definition.

Chapter 8 Writing Assumptions, Limitations, and Delimitations

___ 8.1 When stating an assumption, consider providing the reason(s) why it was necessary to make the assumption.

___ 8.2 If there is a reason for believing that an assumption is true, state the reason.

___ 8.3 If an assumption is highly questionable, consider casting it as a limitation.

____ 8.4 Consider speculating on the possible effects of a limitation on the results of a study.

____ 8.5 Discuss limitations and delimitations separately.

____ 8.6 If a study is seriously flawed by important limitations, consider labeling it as a pilot study.

Chapter 9 Writing Method Sections

____ 9.1 Decide whether to use the term *subjects* or *participants* to refer to the individuals studied.

____ 9.2 Describe the informed consent procedures, if any, as well as steps taken to maintain confidentiality.

____ 9.3 The participants should be described in enough detail for the reader to visualize them.

____ 9.4 When a sample is very small, consider providing a description of individual participants.

____ 9.5 A population should be named, and if only a sample was studied, the method of sampling should be described.

____ 9.6 Explicitly acknowledge weaknesses in sampling.

____ 9.7 Provide detailed information on nonparticipants when possible.

____ 9.8 If there was attrition, state the number who dropped out, the reasons for dropping out, if known, and information on the dropouts, if available.

____ 9.9 Unpublished instruments should be described in detail.

____ 9.10 If a published instrument was used, briefly describe the traits it was designed to measure, its format, and the possible range of score values.

____ 9.11 For both unpublished and published instruments, information on reliability and validity, when available, should be reported.

____ 9.12 Experimental procedures, equipment, and other mechanical matters should be described in sufficient detail so that the study can be replicated.

Chapter 10 Writing Analysis and Results Sections

____ 10.1 Organize the analysis and results section around the research hypotheses, purposes, or questions stated in the introduction.

____ 10.2 Standard statistical procedures need only be named; it is usually not necessary to show formulas or calculations.

____ 10.3 The scores of individual participants usually are not shown; instead, statistics based on the scores should be reported.

____ 10.4 Present descriptive statistics first.

____ 10.5 Organize large numbers of statistics in tables, and give each table a number and descriptive title (i.e., caption).

____ 10.6 When describing the statistics presented in a table, point out only the highlights.

___ 10.7   Statistical figures (i.e., drawings such as bar graphs) should be professionally drawn and used sparingly in journal articles.

___ 10.8   Statistical symbols should be underlined or italicized.

___ 10.9   Use the proper case for each statistical symbol.

___ 10.10 Spell out numbers that are less than ten. Spell out numbers that start sentences.

___ 10.11 Qualitative results should be organized and the organization made clear to the reader.

Chapter 11 Writing Discussion Sections

___ 11.1   Consider starting the discussion with a summary.

___ 11.2   Early in the discussion section, refer to the research hypotheses, purposes, or questions stated in the introduction.

___ 11.3   Point out whether results of the current study are consistent with the results and theories described in the introduction.

___ 11.4   Consider interpreting the results and offering explanations for them in the discussion section.

___ 11.5   Mention important strengths and limitations in the discussion.

___ 11.6   It is usually inappropriate to introduce new data or new references in the discussion section.

___ 11.7   When possible, state specific implications in the discussion section.

___ 11.8   Be specific when making recommendations for future research.

Chapter 12 Writing Abstracts

___ 12.1   In the abstract, refer to the research hypotheses, purposes, or questions.

___ 12.2   Highlights of the methodology should be summarized.

___ 12.3   Highlights of the results should be included in the abstract.

___ 12.4   If a study is based on a theory, name the theory in the abstract.

___ 12.5   An abstract should usually be short; however, there are exceptions.

Chapter 13 A Closer Look at Writing Reports of Qualitative Research

___ 13.1   Consider using the term "qualitative" in the title or abstract of the report.

___ 13.2   Consider discussing the choice of qualitative over quantitative methodology.

___ 13.3   Describe the qualitative method or approach used in the research.

___ 13.4   Consider "revealing yourself" to your reader.

___ 13.5   Avoid calling a sample "purposive" if it is actually a sample of convenience.

___ 13.6   If a purposive sample was used, state the basis for selection of participants.

___ 13.7   Describe how participants were recruited.

___ 13.8   Provide demographic information.

____ 13.9   Provide specific information on data collection methods.

____ 13.10 Describe steps taken to ensure the trustworthiness of the data.

____ 13.11 Provide a specific description of the method of analysis.

____ 13.12 If two or more researchers participated in analyzing the data, describe how they arrived at a consensus.

____ 13.13 In the results section of a qualitative report, provide quantitative results on quantitative matters.

____ 13.14 Consider using the major themes as subheadings in the results section.

____ 13.15 If quotations are reported, consider stating the basis for their selection.

____ 13.16 Consider discussing alternative interpretations of the data and why they were rejected.

Chapter 14 Preparing a Reference List

____ 14.1   Select a style manual and carefully follow its directions for preparing a reference list.

____ 14.2   A journal title is treated like a book title; either underline or italicize it.

____ 14.3   While volume numbers are important in identifying a journal article, issue numbers are not.

____ 14.4   Double-check punctuation in accordance with the style manual.

____ 14.5   Double-check capitalization in accordance with the style manual.

____ 14.6   A reference list should contain entries only for those that have been cited in the research report.

____ 14.7   Cross-check reference citations in the body of the report with those in the reference list.

Notes:

Appendix B

Thinking Straight and Writing That Way[1]

Ann Robinson
University of Arkansas at Little Rock

Everyone who submits manuscripts to top-flight journals gets rejected by the reviewers more than once in his or her publishing career. Often the rejections seem, at best, inexplicable and, at worst, biased. Rejections sting.

In a cooler moment, the disappointed author looks over the rejected paper and tries to read the reviewers' comments more calmly. What do journal reviewers look for in a manuscript? What makes a submission publishable? How can you increase the likelihood that your work will be accepted? These are good questions for any would-be author —seasoned or new—to ask.

In general, sessions on publishing "how-to's" rarely get beyond the obligatory lecture on the importance of the idea. We are told that if the idea is good, we should carry out the research study and proceed to submit the work for publication. If the how-to-get-published session gets past the point of explaining that a good study is one that asks an important question, then we are told that a publishable study is one that is reasonably free of design flaws. It seems to me that these two points ought to be considered givens. Although it is not always easy to think of a good idea, translate it into a researchable question, and design a competent study, most of us already understand the importance of these things. What we want to know now is how to increase our chances of getting competent work published.

Over the last eight years, I have developed the following questions to use when reviewing research manuscripts. They are offered as one

---

[1] Originally published in *Gifted Child Quarterly*, *32*, 367–369 as "Thinking Straight and Writing That Way: Publishing in *Gifted Child Quarterly*." Copyright 1988 by the National Association for Gifted Children. Reprinted with permission.

reviewer's "test" of the publishability of a manuscript and may be helpful as guides for the prospective author.

Reviewer Question 1: What's the point?

Early on in the first "quick read," I ask why I should be interested in this manuscript. Will this study fill a gap in the existing literature? Will this study reconcile apparently contradictory research results from studies already published? Is this study anchored to a real problem affecting the education and upbringing of children and youth? Is this study "newsworthy"? Does the author convince me in the first few paragraphs that this manuscript is going to present important information new to the field or be investigated from a fresh perspective?

The manuscripts that most effectively make their "point" often have brief introductions that state the essence of the issue in the first or last sentence of the first or second paragraph. As a reviewer, I look for that "essence of issue" sentence. It is a benchmark for clear thinking and writing.

Reviewer Question 2: Can I find the general research question?

Reviewer Question 2 is related to the first, but I am now looking for something a bit more technical. The general research question should be stated clearly, and it should serve as the lodestone for the specific questions generated for the study. Congruence is important here. If I were to take each of these specific questions and check them against the general question, I would easily see the connection. For example, in a study of the family systems of underachieving males, the general question is, "What are the interactional relationships within families of gifted students?" (Green, Fine, & Tollefson, 1988). Two specific questions derived from the general one are:

> (1) Is there a difference in the proportion of families of achieving and underachieving gifted students that are classified as functional and dysfunctional? (2) Do family members having achieving or underachieving gifted students differ in their satisfaction with their families? (p. 268).

The manuscripts that most effectively answered Reviewer Question 2 placed the general question at the end of the review of the literature. It will be stated as a question and prefaced with a lead-in like "the general purpose of this study" or "an important research question is." Then the specific questions for the study are enumerated and set apart in a list. The combination of text and visual cues makes it difficult for the reviewer to overlook the focus of the manuscript.

Reviewer Question 3: Can I get a "picture" of the participants of this study?

The appropriate level of description for the participants is difficult to judge. However, it is better to over- rather than underdescribe them. This is true whether the study is experimental or a naturalistic inquiry. Insufficient information about the participants in the study leaves the reviewer wondering if the conclusions are suspect. Would the results be the same if other participants had participated? Go beyond the breakdowns by age or grade, sex, and ethnicity. If the participants are students in a gifted program, describe the identification procedure. If the participants are school personnel, describe their professional positions, years in service, or other variables that might affect the results. As a reviewer, I always try to determine the extent to which a participant sample is volunteer and how seriously volunteerism might bias the results. If a study is conducted in one school building, district, or one teacher or parent advocate group, I look for descriptions of this context. How large is the school or organization? Is it rural, urban, or suburban? Who is responding to surveys? Fathers or mothers? Are families intact, single parent, or extended? What is the socioeconomic level?

For example, in a study of learning styles, Ricca (1984) included the following information to give a thorough picture of the subjects.

> The study population included 425 students in grades four, five, and six from one city school and one suburban school district in Western New York. Descriptive contrast groups represented participants who were identified as gifted and a contrast group taken from the remaining general school students available. Gifted students were identified by a multidimensional screening process with data sources indicated in Table 1 (p. 121).

This information is followed by a further explanation of the identification process and three brief tables that provide a tidy summary of student demographics and cognitive and academic characteristics. The combination of text and tables gives the reviewer a clear picture of the participants in the study.

The reviewer may ultimately ask the author to trim the text on participants, but overzealous descriptions serve two purposes. First, they demonstrate to the reviewer that the author is a careful worker. Second, they rein in generalizations, which appear in the Conclusions and

Implications sections of the manuscript. An author may well be entitled to make statements about the population from which the sample of participants is drawn, but if the demographics of the group change, the conclusions may not be safely generalized.

The manuscripts that most effectively create a picture of their sample include the basics like age, grade, sex, and ethnicity succinctly, sometimes in tabled form. Case study researchers are less likely to use tables because of smaller samples, but they do identify the reasons why they believe a participant is representative of a large group. In studies of gifted children, the most effective manuscripts clearly state the selection procedure and identify specific instruments or checklists, if appropriate, under the Participants section of the paper.

Reviewer Question 4: Is this author killing flies with an elephant gun?

As a reviewer, I examine the manuscript for a comfortable fit among the research questions, the kinds of data that have been collected, and the tools of analysis. In the case of manuscripts that present quantitative data and statistical analyses, I apply Occam's razor. The simplest statistics are usually the best. A good research question can be insightfully investigated with relatively simple analyses provided the assumptions are not too badly violated. The purpose of statistics is to summarize and clarify, not to fog.

Of course, authors who seek to control confounded variables through the use of more sophisticated statistical treatments like the currently popular LISREL increase the likelihood that multiple causation is disentangled. We certainly gain from technological innovation; however, the key is to determine if the impetus for the study is a substantive research question or a fascination with the newest techniques.

The manuscripts that answer Reviewer Question 4 most effectively are those in which hypotheses do not sink under the weight of the analyses. As I read the Design and Analysis sections, am I able to keep my eye on the important variables? A good indicator is a sentence in the Design section that gives me the rationale for using quite sophisticated or new statistical and qualitative techniques. For example, a study of ethnic differences in a mathematics program for gifted students included the following explanation for the selection of a specialized kind of regression analysis (Robinson, Bradley, & Stanley, in review):

> Regression discontinuity is a quasi-experimental design that allows the experimenter to test for treatment effects without a randomized control group and the attendant withholding of services. This a priori design statistically controls for prior differences by using the identification variable along with program participation (status) as independent variables in a multiple regression model (p. 7).

Another indication that the study is being driven by its questions rather than its statistics is the author's effort to make connecting statements between a technique and its interpretation. To return to the previous regression example:

> If the associated t test of the regression coefficient is significant, it is indicative of a program that impacts on its participants (p. 7).

Reviewer Question 5: Would George Orwell approve?

Dogging the reviewer through both the "quick read" and the "close read" of the manuscript is the ease with which the author has answered the first four questions. If we look back at those questions, we see the common thread of clarity running through them. What is the point? Where is the question? Who is this study about? Does the analysis illuminate rather than obfuscate?

Reviewer Question 5 is the final test. Would George Orwell approve? In 1946, Orwell published "Politics and the English Language," one of the clearest statements on writing effectively ever to appear in print. The thesis of his essay was that "modern English, especially written English, is full of bad habits, which spread by imitation and which can be avoided if one is willing to take the necessary trouble . . . prose consists less and less of words chosen for the sake of their meaning, and more and more of phrases tacked together like sections of a prefabricated hen-house" (p. 159). Orwell was clearly unhappy with vague writing and professional jargon. He felt that poor writing was an indication of sloppy thinking, and he excused neither the social scientist nor the novelist from his strict dicta of good, vigorous writing. He had a particular dislike of using ready-made phrases like "lay the foundation," and he was equally appalled at the indiscriminate use of scientific terms to give the impression of objectivity to biased statements.

As a reviewer, I apply Orwell's tough rules to the test of every manuscript I receive. It means that the manuscript author has answered Reviewer Questions 1 through 4 successfully.

According to Orwell, "the following rules will cover most cases:

1. Never use a metaphor, simile, or other figure of speech that you are used to seeing in print.
2. Never use a long word where a short one will do.
3. If it is possible to cut a word out, always cut it out.
4. Never use the passive where you can use the active.
5. Never use a foreign phrase, a scientific word, or a jargon word if you can think of an everyday English equivalent.
6. Break any of these rules sooner than say anything outright 'barbarous'" (p. 170).

Orwell had the good sense to include the sixth rule as a disclaimer. All writers make errors and violate rules, sometimes out of carelessness, sometimes for effect. It is also true that writing for highly specialized journals does require the judicious use of technical language, just as sheep shearers need specialized terms to describe differing grades of wool. However, moderation in the use and the arbitrary, spontaneous creation of specialized vocabulary is certainly warranted in our field. It is refreshing to read an author who states that the subjects in the study are "thinking critically" rather than "realizing greater cognitive gains."

Orwell makes many fine points about the importance of sincerity in thinking and writing. For the prospective social science writer, none are more important than the careful selection and lively use of technical terms. I know of no more rigorous test to apply to a manuscript than to ask if George Orwell would approve. Passing this "test" means the author is thinking straight and writing that way.

References

Green, K., Fine, M. J., & Tollefson, N. (1988). Family systems characteristics and underachieving gifted adolescent males. *Gifted Child Quarterly, 32*, 267–276.

Orwell, G. (1953). Politics and the English language. In G. Orwell (Ed.), *A Collection of Essays* (pp. 156–171). San Diego: Harcourt, Brace, Jovanovich.

Rica, J. (1984). Learning styles and preferred instructional strategies. *Gifted Child Quarterly, 28*, 121–126.

Robinson, A., Bradley, R., & Stanley, T. D. (in review). Opportunity to achieve: The identification and performance of Black students in a program for the mathematically talented.

Appendix C

The Null Hypothesis and Significance Testing[1]

Formal significance testing begins with the *null hypothesis*. This is a statistical hypothesis that asserts that any differences we observe when studying random samples are the result of random (chance) errors created by the random sampling. For example, suppose you asked a random sample of men from some population and a random sample of women from the same population whether they support legalizing physician-assisted suicide for the terminally ill and found that 51% of the women supported it while only 49% of the men supported it. At first, you might be tempted to report that women are more supportive of this proposition than men. However, the null hypothesis warns us that the 2-percentage-point difference between women and men may have resulted solely from sampling errors. In other words, there may be no difference between men and women in the population—we may have found a difference because we administered our questionnaire to only these two particular samples.

Of course, it is also possible that the men and women in the population are truly different in their opinion on physician-assisted suicide and the population difference is responsible for the difference between the percentages for the two samples. In other words, the samples may accurately reflect the gender difference in the population. This possibility is called an *alternative hypothesis* (i.e., an alternative to the null hypothesis).

Which hypothesis is correct? It turns out that the only way to answer this question is to test the null hypothesis. If the test indicates that we may reject the null hypothesis, then we will be left with only the alternative hypothesis as an explanation. When we reject the null hypothesis, we say that we have identified a *reliable* difference—one we can rely on because it probably is not just an artifact of random errors.

Through a set of computational procedures that are beyond the scope of this book, a significance test results in a *probability that the null*

---

[1] The authors are grateful to Mildred L. Patten, who wrote this appendix.

hypothesis is true. The symbol for this probability is *p*. By conventional standards, when the probability that the null hypothesis is true is as low as or lower than 5 in 100, we reject the null hypothesis. (Note that a low probability means that it is unlikely that the null hypothesis is true. If something is *unlikely* to be true, we reject it as a possibility.)

The formal term that researchers use when discussing the rejection of the null hypothesis is *statistical significance*. For example, the following two statements might appear in the results section of a research report:

"The difference between the means for the liberals and conservatives is statistically significant ($p < .05$)."

"The difference between the means for the men and women is not statistically significant ($p > .05$)."

The first statement says that the probability that the null hypothesis is true is less than ($<$) 5 in 100; thus, the null hypothesis is rejected, and the difference is declared to be *statistically significant*. The second statement says that the probability that the null hypothesis is true is greater than ($>$) 5 in 100; thus, the null hypothesis is *not* rejected, and the difference is *not statistically significant*.

In other words, significance tests are helping us make decisions based on the odds that something is true. We all do this in everyday life. For example, when you prepare to cross a busy street, you look at oncoming cars to judge their speed and distance to see if it is safe to cross. If you decide that there is a *low probability* that you will be able to cross the street safely, you *reject* the hypothesis that it is safe to cross the street.

Notes:

Notes:

Notes:

Notes: